WHAT IS LOVE?

The Bible on Broadway

Sonia Harrison Jones

WHAT IS LOVE?

The Bible on Broadway

EP

Erser & Pond

Cover design by Benjamin Beaumont
Front cover photo ©iStockphoto/Liliboas
Back cover photo ©TerryJAlcorn
Illustrations ©Microsoft Clip Art, except where otherwise noted

Printed in the U.S.A. by Erser & Pond Publishers, Ltd.
1096 Queen St., Suite 225, Halifax, N.S., Canada B3H 2R9

Library and Archives Canada Cataloguing in Publication

Jones, Sonia, author
    What is love? : the Bible on Broadway / Sonia Harrison Jones.

ISBN 978-0-9865683-9-8 (pbk.)

    1. Bible--Study and teaching. 2. Theater--Religious aspects--
Christianity. 3. Music theater--History and criticism. I. Title.

BS600.3.J65 2013   220.071   C2013-902638-X

This book is dedicated
to all those who have loved.

And remember a truth that once was spoken:
to love another person is to see the face of God.

—Les Misérables, the musical

Table of Contents

Footnote: Since the publisher's many pleas for permission to quote songs from the three musicals were ignored, it was felt that the best way around the problem was to summarize the content of the songs for the reader's benefit. The interested readers are encouraged to purchase the CD or DVD of the musicals, where the lyrics perhaps may be found. Many of the songs and lyrics are available on You Tube as well.

A Musical Trilogy

Meditations on the Nature of Love

Phantom of the Opera: **The Chiaroscuro of Love**

This seven-chapter study is the first of a series of three topical meditations on the nature of love. We shall begin with a brief review of love in its historical perspective, then we'll take a look at *The Phantom of the Opera,* based on a novel by Gaston Leroux (1868-1927) with music by Andrew Lloyd Webber and lyrics by Charles Hart, to see where it fits into the wide spectrum of confusing but heart-warming emotions commonly known as "love."

As we study *The Phantom of the Opera* we'll notice that the main character, the Phantom, is quite the old *roué,* and certainly a past master at the art of seduction. He assures Christine that if she surrenders herself to him, he will teach her to *live as she has never lived before* as they dance to the *music of the night.*

A mixture of Don Juan, the Serpent, and the touching figure of the Beast in *Beauty and the Beast,* the Phantom of the Opera will provide us with much food for discussion.

Man of La Mancha: **Transformational Love**

Don Quixote de la Mancha, the main character in the famous Spanish masterpiece by Miguel de Cervantes (1547-1616), has been recreated as the hero of a modern musical play with a book by Dale Wasserman, lyrics by Joe Darion, and music by Mitch Leigh. In this narrative an elderly Spanish country gentleman reads so many novels about knights in shining armor that he eventually decides to emulate his heroes and sally forth into the world to rescue widows, orphans, and damsels in distress.

He creates many strange and humorous situations in his own imagination. He believes, for example, that a certain prostitute whom he encounters in a disreputable inn is really a princess in disguise. He falls hopelessly in love with this hard-nosed woman, who initially believes that he is cruelly making fun of her. But as the story unfolds we discover that Don Quixote's love is actually transforming her and giving her hope for a new life based on her "master's" high ideals.

Les Misérables: Love and Redemption

Finally we shall study *Les Misérables* (based on the literary masterpiece by 19th-century French author Victor Hugo), where we'll meet Jean Valjean, the convict who learns of God's love through the mercy of a priest who saves him from prison. He dedicates his life to helping others as an expression of his gratitude for what God has done for him.

These studies will show us that love is by no means easy to define. It is often as complex and as fraught with hidden agendas as are human beings themselves. The Phantom is a mixture of seducer and lonely Beast, while Don Quixote's delusions are both humorous and divinely noble. We too nurse ambiguous feelings as we wander through the desert on our way home to the God who loves us truly.

Introduction

What on Earth is Love?

All Things to All People?

Anyone trying to discover an all-encompassing definition of love is going to find the task very difficult, if not impossible. Love can be heavenly, or it can seem like hell itself. It can be inspiring or depressing, it can lift the spirits or send them crashing. Love can bring out the best in us, or the worst, or both. It can be ennobling, maddening, gratifying, frightening, or all of these things in sequence or jumbled together. But one thing is certain: love is a complex emotion, and nobody knows quite what to make of it.

Love Among the Ancients

The ancient Greeks were so aware of the complexity of love that they developed various different words to describe it. It would take us too far off the track to examine them all, but three might suffice for our purposes. *Aphros* is a word for love which emphasizes pure sexual desire and gratification primarily for its own sake. The goddess Aphrodite derives her name from this word, as does *aphrodisiac*. In today's vernacular one might use this term to describe the kind of transient love that takes place in a one-night stand, where there is little interest in knowing the partner on a deep level.

Love between the sexes in the ancient world was often (but certainly not always) a matter of this kind of sensual gratification. The Roman poet Ovid, for example, wrote bold and bawdy tales describing the sexual exploits of the gods. Many centuries later the English poet Chaucer wrote equally ribald tales, as did the French author Rabelais and countless others up through the present day.

It could be said that *aphros* is located so far to one end of the spectrum that it doesn't really qualify as love at all. We can't completely disregard it, however, because sexual expression can be a beautiful part of certain other aspects of love. Yet if we separate *aphros* from these other kinds of love and if we engage in it only for its own sake (or, more truthfully, for *our* own sake), then we are probably talking about what is now usually referred to as "recreational sex," an activity that is enjoying a renaissance or perhaps even an apogée today.

The Early Christians

We mentioned a second type of love that inspired the ancient Greeks, and this was called *agape* (spiritual love). It first existed between educated, aristocratic men who enjoyed an intellectual and spiritual relationship with each other. It also existed between older men who mentored young men in the joys of intellectual exploration and attainment. Women were thought to have little capacity for such matters, however, and were therefore not usually the focus of agape love.

But Jesus changed all that. As a result of his teachings, women were elevated not to a wobbly pedestal (a position imposed on them by the troubadours twelve centuries later), but to a state of true equality with men. Women and men became partners in helping one another and in serving the Lord. In this fertile ground a new kind of agape took root which led to deeper fulfillment in marriage.

The Twelfth-Century Troubadours

In the twelfth century the old concept of the forbidden fruit was popularized in a third form of love that was also known to the Greeks, which they called *eros* (after Eros, the son of Aphrodite, the goddess of love). The troubadours in the south of France rediscovered the idea that desire can be greatly enhanced if the object of that desire is unobtainable. Hence these bards dedicated themselves to pursuing the wives of powerful noblemen (who tried to protect them from their ardent and persistent suitors by keeping them locked up in turrets), preferably highly-born ladies whose favors would have been more difficult to win.

Some of the best music and poetry of the age resulted from the plaintive strumming of the lovesick troubadours who were hoping, usually in vain, to win the hearts of these beautiful but merciless ladies. This soon led to what is now known as "chivalric love," another form of *eros* that was practiced by the more "manly" and less artistically-inclined knights who sought to win the favor of equally unobtainable ladies through heroic exploits and acts of bravery in order to be worthy of winning their hearts.

Where the Greeks were concerned, *eros* was sometimes viewed as a kind of aberration, as in Euripides' *Phaedra,* a tragedy that in some ways brings to mind the movie *Fatal Attraction.* Phaedra's passionate love for her husband's son eventually drives her mad.

The twelfth-century interpretation of *eros* added a new twist: men and women who were intoxicated by passionate love were no longer seen as candidates for the loony bin—instead they were admired for their heroic willingness to embrace the tragic consequences of their passionate love for the sake of the beloved (or more likely for the sake of the exciting and powerful feelings engendered by the situation itself). Be that as it may, the popularity of *eros* was firmly established in the twelfth century and has remained a huge box office draw to this day.

BIBLE POINTER

The best description of Christian agape love is found in 1 Corinthians:13. The Apostle Paul adds some suggestions on how husbands and wives should behave toward one another in Ephesians 5:22-28, and the words of Jesus in Mark 12:29 concerning the greatest commandment remain unsurpassed.

The Dynamics of Passionate Love

Most of the poets and lovers of the last eight centuries were consciously or unconsciously aware that *eros* cannot be kept alive unless it is carefully nurtured in the world of the imagination. As we mentioned before, it is essential that the beloved be as unobtainable as possible, and that an endless series of obstacles be erected to prevent the consummation of the lover's yearnings. This is achieved throughout literature by variations on three basic plots:

- **Don Juan:** This dashing Spanish *caballero* (like his Italian counterpart, Casanova) pursues women with feverish determination, but as soon as he wins them over he loses interest and moves on to the next one.

- **Tristan and Isolde:** The brooding protagonist of this ancient legend concentrates his efforts on wooing an unobtainable lady, enjoying her favors only very infrequently so that he may have plenty of time to dream of her. When she draws too close he creates obstacles to keep her at arm's length.

- **Novels of Chivalry:** The knight-errant in these tales often confines his love to a woman he has created in his own imagination (one whom he sees gazing out at the world from a distant turret). He can possess her only after many difficult exploits that are carried out to impress her and win her favor.

The View of the Church

At first it may not seem surprising to us that the ancients failed to take passionate love seriously. How, then, could *eros* have dug its roots so deeply into the social and spiritual fabric of the last eight centuries? The troubadours describe it as a profoundly ennobling emotion that inspires the lover to accomplish great deeds, while at the same time it offers him a transcendent experience of the highest order. Nothing provides a greater sense of fulfillment and meaning in life, say the devotees of *eros*, than the excitement of this kind of love, which acts as a powerfully addictive narcotic to the one who is enslaved by its magic.

Fulfillment? Meaning? Excitement? The Church saw the dangers inherent in an activity that demanded an individual's total commitment and which promised a fulfillment it was unable to deliver. *Eros* was akin to a religion, and a heretical one at that. It is no wonder that Christian authorities were eager to stamp out the flock's growing infatuation with the new heresy. In the next few chapters we shall examine the methods of a particularly seductive character: The Phantom of the Opera. But we must step gingerly, for as we have seen, *eros* can be a shimmering yet ever-fascinating mirage.

The Phantom

of the

Opera

THE CHIAROSCURO OF LOVE

Chapter One

Keeping Passion Alive

Plot Summary: *Phantom of the Opera* (1)

Prologue: The Paris Opera House, 1911

An auction is in progress on the stage of the Opera House. The elderly Raoul is making bids for items from performances of an opera that took place long ago. An antique chandelier is presented for bidding (Lot 666), and we are suddenly swept back to the time when Raoul was a young man and the chandelier hung in splendor from the dome of the Opera House.

Act One: Paris, 1881

A new opera, Hannibal, is being rehearsed, and the prima donna, Carlotta, is on center stage. As she sings, a back-drop falls on her suddenly, almost killing her. Nobody can explain how this accident took place, although some say it must have been the work of "the ghost."

> Galled by this apparent attempt on her life, Carlotta storms out, leaving the production without a leading lady. In recent days there have been, she declares huffily as she exits, too many such "accidents." Madame Giry, the ballet mistress, gives the managers a note from the "ghost," who demands a salary and a complimentary opera box.

Song Summary

Think of Me

Christine Daae, one of the main dancers at the Paris Opera, attends the audition for Carlotta's part. Christine has been taking singing lessons, but is unwilling to say from whom. She decides to sing *Think of Me*, a song from *Hannibal*. As she sings, the young Raoul, now an enthusiastic patron of the Paris Opera, is entranced by her talented performance.

After the show, an eerie voice is heard coming from the rafters. It's the Phantom of the Opera, also singing *Think of Me*, in which he implores Christine to remember him fondly when they say goodbye. He knows she wants her freedom— he only asks that she remember all the good things they've shared and seen, and not dwell on the things that might have been. He reminds her that they never said their love was evergreen or as unchanging as the sea, but he tells her there will never be a day when he won't think of her. Christine echoes his words, assuring him that she feels the same way.

Commentary

Hannibal crosses the Alps

Rome has declared war on Carthage (the Second Punic War: 218-201 B.C.) and Hannibal, the Carthaginian general, is preparing to invade Italy in reaction to the challenge. The Queen of Carthage, who is in love with Hannibal in this play within a play, provides forty elephants and other military supplies to help ensure the victory of Hannibal's army. Later he crosses the Alps with the elephants, making his invasion of Italy one of the most remarkable feats in military history.

In this scene Hannibal assembles his soldiers, horses, and elephants and sets off to conquer Italy. The Queen of Carthage (played by Christine) is in love with Hannibal in this story, and she sings an aria in which she asks him to remember her while he is away.

One can imagine the scene: Hannibal, astride a spirited horse, looking handsome in his military uniform, graciously accepting the adulation of the crowds while the Queen, aloof and beautiful, surveys her lover's glory. He is the salvation of his fellow countrymen and she is the noble monarch, trembling with sorrow as she contemplates their imminent separation.

Questions

1 What elements in the foregoing description set the stage for *eros*?

2 What aspects of Christine's song help us to know that the Queen's love for Hannibal is passionate (or romantic)?

3 Why do you think this particular opera, *Hannibal*, was introduced as a play within the play?

4 What can we deduce about the Phantom so far? What qualities does he have that seem "devilish"?

5 Extra credit: Would you say that King David's love for Bathsheba was inspired by *eros* or by *agape*? Why? (See 2 Samuel, chapters 11 and 12)

NOTABLE QUOTES

If the Devil doesn't exist, but man has created him, he has created him in his own image and likeness.

—Dostoyevski, *The Brothers Karamazov*

©iStockphoto/LindaMarieB

Chapter Two

The Great Imitator

Plot Summary: *Phantom of the Opera* (2)

Christine's friend Meg asks her about her mysterious voice teacher, but Christine can only tell her that he is the "angel of music" which her late father had always promised would come to her after he died. She has heard his voice, but she has never yet seen him.

Raoul joins Christine backstage to congratulate her on the splendid performance she gave. The meeting becomes a reunion, for they both realize that long ago they used to play together as children. Raoul invites Christine to dinner, and leaves to get his coat.

While Christine awaits Raoul's return, the strange voice is heard again. Suddenly a figure appears behind the mirror —it is the Phantom, the teacher she's never seen, her Angel of Music, his face half obscured by a white mask.

He is in a rage about Raoul's daring to take a personal interest in his protégée.

Meanwhile, Christine tells Meg that her father once spoke of an angel of music, and she can sense his closeness to her as he calls to her softly.

Song Summary

Angel of Music

For Christine the Phantom is an unseen genius, an Angel of Music, a guide and a guardian. She begs him to grant her his glory, but he is furious with Raoul, who has audaciously taken it upon himself to bask in Christine's glory. She asks the Phantom to forgive her and enter into her. The Phantom is flattered, and tells her to look in the mirror, where she'll find him waiting. Once again Christine sings to her mentor, asking him to grant her his glory. She further asks him to step out of the mirror and show himself to her.

Angel of Music, hide no longer, she implores him. *Come to me, strange angel...*

Commentary

The hidden predator

It is hard for us nowadays to speak of Satan with a straight face. He seems like a throwback to the days of witch-hunts and superstition. If he exists at all, he is either a cop-out *(the devil made me do it),* or the bogeyman of our childhood.

This is exactly the way he wants it, of course. It suits his purposes for us to let down our guard as we wander through life. He remains carefully hidden as he holds out the bait for our eager inspection, for we should remember that he aspires to be the consummate fisher of men.

A connoisseur of human nature

A good fisherman or trapper spends most of his waking hours studying his prey. He knows their daily habits, where they congregate, and what kind of bait appeals most to the different types of victims. Satan, too, knows we hunger and thirst, and he is eager to provide us with an *ersatz* substitute for living water and the bread of life. He also knows we have a "God-shaped hole" in our hearts that must be filled with his spirit if we are to find joy, meaning, and fulfillment in life. Yet all too often we open ourselves to bad influences in the misguided hope that we'll find joy in all the wrong places.

Cloud Nine

Excitement, meaning, fulfillment. Do those words ring a bell? In the prologue we discussed how we are sometimes tempted to satisfy these yearnings by throwing ourselves recklessly into the arms of *eros*. You smile? You, of course, are not the reckless type. But Broadway musicals, Italian opera, Hollywood films, and romantic novels continue to attract people everywhere.

We're a bit ashamed of showing too much enthusiasm, mind you, because we wouldn't want our friends to suspect that we were soppy or sentimental or maybe a little soft in the head. Yet what can be more glorious than new love? We're on cloud nine, we want to shout it from the roof tops. We're ten feet tall, we're ready to conquer the world, we feel fully alive... until the bubble bursts.

The artful deceiver

Bubbles bursting? We'll have none of that. It's a rare lover who can bring himself to imagine that his love might not be lasting and true. We tend to believe that we have never met anyone quite like the beloved, and Satan is all too willing to encourage this illusion, as well as many others like it.

Why are trout so hard to catch? Because they are smart. Of all the game fish, they are the best at hiding, they are the most suspicious of bait, and they are the first of all their brethren to recognize hip boots when they see them. We must learn to know the enemy too, for our defense can also be enhanced by being alert to his schemes and ploys.

We would do well to remember that Satan is not only a deceiver and a liar. His greatest triumph is to take our best qualities and pervert them (maybe only just a little) so that we end up missing the mark altogether. God filled our hearts with the capacity to love nobly and deeply and truly, but perhaps this potential in our nature is exactly the quality that most infuriates Satan, because it is the very essence of God, who is love itself. It is love that draws us to God, and it is love that created us and the universe. How appropriate, then, that Satan should want to concentrate on destroying the beauty of this love by perverting it from its intended goal!

Eros cast us down, but A*gape* overcame the world

Unlike the humble trout, we have a God who lives within us. Although Satan would love to slip into our hearts too, he can only do so if we invite him in and make room for him.

It would be unthinkable, of course, for a Christian to do this knowingly, for we are not consciously attracted to Satan. But as fallen human beings, we often take the wrong path. At the risk of drawing too many conclusions too early in our series of studies, we should remind ourselves that when we yield to temptation we are questioning God's will for our lives. When we choose to stand on our own personal cloud nine, we are failing to trust God to know what is best for us.

Questions

1 What parallels do you see between the Holy Spirit and the Phantom's imitation of him as described in the song?
2 Why is Christine attracted to the Phantom? What does he offer her? Why is she frightened of him?
3 What kind of character does the Phantom reveal here?
4 What significance does the mirror have?

Chapter Three

Seduction in the Dark

Plot Summary: *Phantom of the Opera* (3)

The mirror in Christine's dressing room glides open and the Phantom draws her into the dark beyond. He punts her across a lake in a boat (like Charon taking dead souls over the River Styx), into his subterranean "lair." He explains the purpose of the voice lessons: he is a composer, and she is to sing the music that inspires him.

Song Summaries

The Phantom of the Opera

Christine finds herself in a dreamlike state as the Phantom takes her toward his watery lair in the bowels of the Opera House. He boasts that his power over her is growing ever stronger, and even if she turns away from him and glances nervously behind, he will still remain close to her, inside her mind. Christine realizes that he is using her beauty as a sort of mask to hide his ugliness. The Phantom is annoyed by this insight, and he reminds her that it's *his* voice that the people come to hear. Meanwhile some off-stage guards from the Opera House chatter nervously as they pursue the Phantom through the dark labyrinth to his underground lair.

The Music of the Night

But to the Phantom his home hardly qualifies as a "lair." To him it is a kingdom where his music reigns supreme. As far as he's concerned, Christine has only one purpose in life, and that is to serve him and to accompany his music with her heavenly voice. He describes the dark night as a vehicle to sharpen Christine's senses and awaken her imagination. He encourages her to turn her face away from the garish light of day, and abandon herself to the music of the night.

He sounds almost like a cult leader as he instructs her to forget the life she knew previously so she can live more fully at his side. He promises to give her the ecstasy of being enveloped by beautiful music in the darkness that she knows she cannot fight. She can only belong to him if she allows her soul to take her where she yearns to be. He finishes his seductive song by advising her to let her darker side give in to the power of the music that he writes. Then, as a final touch, he flatters her by assuring her that she alone can make his soul take flight, so he needs her to help him create the music of the night.

Commentary

A still, small voice

The word *seduction* derives from the Latin "seducere," *to lead astray*. Notice the accuracy of the meaning in English: we are being *led* down the garden path—we are not forced to go against our will. Notice, too, that when we go astray the clear implication is that we are wandering off in the wrong direction, like sheep that have lost their way.

As you reread the description of the songs on the previous pages, keep in mind that we all tend to believe that the grass is greener on the other side of the fence. Many people also sympathize with Robert Frost when he says "something there is that doesn't love a wall..." (or a fence, as the case may be).

Darkness and light

Where does the wrong direction take us? The Bible often describes it as a kingdom of darkness—a world of mirages, false promises, and counterfeit pleasures. In our fallen state we sometimes feel quite at home bumbling around in this world, grasping at the various carrots and straws that seem forever out of reach. Perhaps under ideal conditions it would not take us very long to realize that God has something much better than an illusory carrot to offer us, but we are usually too occupied with our own desires to listen to *the still, small voice*. We prefer the dramatic, seductive tones of a music that promises us the carrot (or the greener grass) if we agree to follow the Pied Piper away from the light (and over the cliff).

Questions

1 Do you think it is significant that the Phantom of the Opera visits Christine while she is sleeping?
2 Why does Christine turn from him to glance behind?
3 What words in this song describe how the Phantom and Christine have merged together?
4 Why is a "labyrinth" such an appropriate description of the pathways of the kingdom of darkness? How does the Bible describe the path that leads to the kingdom of light?
5 According to the Phantom's opening words, what must the subjects of his kingdom do? What kind of music is he referring to?
6 In what ways does the Phantom expect Christine to imitate the work of Christians in the kingdom of heaven?

7　How does the Phantom describe the darkness versus the light? Does his description tally with the Bible's view? How about your own view?

8　What does the Phantom exhort Christine to do? What does he promise her if she obeys?

9　Why might she be tempted to do so? Do you think that you would you be tempted, too?

BIBLE QUOTE

[11] … And, behold, the LORD passed by, and a great and strong wind rent the mountains, and broke in pieces the rocks before the LORD; but the LORD was not in the wind: and after the wind an earthquake; but the LORD was not in the earthquake:

[12] And after the earthquake a fire; but the LORD was not in the fire: and after the fire a still small voice.

—1 Kings 19:11-13, King James Version (KJV)

NOTABLE QUOTES

"Religion is an illusion, and it derives its strength from the fact that it falls in with our instinctual desires."
　　　　　　　—Sigmund Freud, "Philosophy of Life"

Chapter Four

True Love to the Rescue?

Plot Summary: *Phantom of the Opera (4)*

The Phantom is seated at his organ in his lair at dawn, composing music. When Christine awakens, she is overcome with curiosity and rips the mask from his face. He curses her and says that now she will never again be free.

Although she is scared, Christine still has the courage to contemplate his unmasked face. The Phantom seems to admire this, and he softens a little. He claims her fear will turn to love when she finally learns to understand him. He describes himself as a loathsome beast which burns in hell but secretly yearns for heaven.

Christine returns to the opera company, where she is now participating in a new production. The Phantom is enraged because she has not been given the leading role, so he kills one of the singers. Christine flees to the roof in fear and panic, where she is joined by Raoul.

Song Summary

All I Ask of You

Raoul assures Christine that she need not fear the darkness anymore, for he will protect her. Christine asks him to assure her that he loves her and to promise that all he says is true—that's all she asks of him. Raoul replies that all he asks of her is that she allow him to go with her anywhere she goes. The Phantom overhears them confess their love for each other, and he is overcome with hurt and anger. He bitterly blames Christine for letting him teach her to sing like an angel, only to betray him by using her beautifully-trained voice to impress Raoul and cause him to fall in love with her. He says that Christine will curse the day that she didn't do everything he asked of her. He then cuts the chandelier loose and it goes crashing down on the audience.

Commentary

The face behind the mask

In the late nineteenth century Oscar Wilde wrote *The Picture of Dorian Gray,* a novel describing the life and adventures of a notorious womanizer in London society. His phenomenal success with the ladies seems partly due to the fact that his face never ages over the years—it remains a mask of youthful charm and unlined innocence. But at the end of the story his portrait is discovered in the attic, revealing the wrinkled features of a cynical, debauched old man... the real man behind the mask.

What about the face of Jesus? The New Testament tells us nothing about what Jesus really looked like, but in the Old Testament we find a very brief description in the prophetic message of Isaiah: "He had no beauty or majesty to attract us to him, nothing in his appearance that we should desire him" (Isaiah 53:2). This passage reminds us to concentrate on the inner qualities of our neighbors rather than allow ourselves to be influenced by the superficial shape or comeliness of the outer "vessel."

Freedom to love

When the Phantom curses Christine for tearing off his mask and declares that from then on she will never be free, he ironically loses all hope of winning her love. But God understood his creatures better. He knew that if we were truly to love him we would have to come to him of our own accord, and he was prepared to risk everything to make this love possible. And when we do, everything else falls into place. Our response to his love is to love him in return, which fills us with the desire to serve him, please him, trust him, obey him, praise him, and to have faith in his plan for our lives. For us it is a taste, or perhaps a foretaste of *agape*, which God nurtures in our hearts when we seek his face.

Questions

1   What do you suppose motivated the Phantom and Dorian Gray to hide their faces? How did this affect their relationship with others?
2   When Christine unmasked the Phantom, what did each of them express and why? Do you think that Christine's discovery affected the way she felt about Raoul?
3   What sort of love do you suppose is most likely to survive an unmasking? Do you believe the Phantom when he tells Christine that her fear will turn to love when she learns to understand him?
4   Do you believe the Phantom when he says that he secretly yearns for heaven?

5 What do Christine and Raoul ask of each other? What, on the other hand, does the Phantom ask of *them?* Compare the quality of their love. What do you think of Christine's comment to Raoul: *"Say the word and I will follow you"?*

6 Compare the freedom promised by the Phantom, and the freedom that Jesus promises us.

7 Comment on the symbolism of the Opera's chandelier that comes crashing down on the audience.

BIBLE QUOTES

Satan is cast out of heaven

How you have fallen from heaven, oh morning star, son of the dawn! You have been cast down to the earth, you who once laid low the nations!

—Isaiah 14:12

The great dragon was hurled down—that ancient serpent called the devil or Satan, who leads the whole earth astray. He was hurled to the earth, and his angels with him.

—Revelation 12:9

He [Jesus] replied, "I saw Satan fall like lightning from heaven."

—Luke 10:18

Freedom under the law

You, my brothers, were called to be free. But do not use your freedom to indulge the sinful nature; rather, serve one another in love. The entire law is summed up in a single command: "Love your neighbor as yourself."

—Galatians 5:13-14

Chapter Five

Never Too Late

Plot Summary: *Phantom of the Opera* (5)

Through violence, threats and murder, the Phantom has succeeded in forcing the director to give Christine the role of Aminta in the new opera that he has written: *Don Juan Triumphant*. The opera is now under way, and in this scene the Phantom kills the singer who plays Don Juan so that he can sing the part himself opposite Christine.

The Phantom is now dressed up as Don Juan—and Don Juan is in turn disguised as a servant as part of an elaborate plan to seduce Aminta.

Song Summary

Past the Point of No Return

The Phantom assures Christine that their passions are now going to fuse and merge, and that in her mind she has already dropped all her defenses and surrendered to him. Moreover she is past the point of no return, and all the games they've played are at an end. He tells her there is no use resisting— she should abandon all thought and let the dream of their love descend, for a sweet seduction now lies before them.

Christine says that she is now at the point where speech has become silent, and she imagines their bodies entwining. She has made up her mind, and she has no second thoughts. She agrees that she is past the point of no return and past all thought of right or wrong.

Christine reveals the Phantom's face to the audience, then he vanishes just as the police arrive. They pull open a curtain upstage, discovering the dead body of the actor whom the Phantom murdered and left hanging by a rope.

Commentary

A triple disguise

The Phantom has now reached a point where his masquerade is becoming a bit more complicated. He has covered his face with not one, but *three* different masks, all calculated to lure Christine into his arms. First he dresses as the servant whom Aminta (Christine) in fact already loves; but behind the servant disguise lurks Don Juan, a highly-skilled seducer who would have frightened Aminta had she known who he really was; and behind the Don Juan disguise we have our friend the Phantom, who has already unwillingly revealed his face to Christine. One almost senses in these disguises a certain despair on the part of the Phantom—all this wizardry suggests the grand finale of a fireworks display erupting in the last hour, with an explosion of different faces appearing and disappearing in the night.

Don Juan triumphant

To complement his many disguises, the Phantom creates music and lyrics for Christine to sing in this dark night of the soul. As did the Serpent of old, he excites her imagination with many promises of heightened intellectual and emotional experiences, and orchestrates her responses with the creative skill of a master musician. He evidently expects to emerge triumphant, but he seems to forget that Christine has already seen through his disguises. He also appears to be oblivious to the fact that Christine is not Aminta—has the Phantom been ensnared by his own fantasies? Christine plays the part of Aminta with convincing professionalism, learned under the tutelage of the Phantom himself... yet it is he who utters a cry of genuine rage when his expected triumph does not come about ("down once more to the dungeon of my black despair, down we plunge to the prison of my mind...").

Questions

1 What arguments does Don Juan use to convince Aminta they should give in to their desire? How does she respond to this? Do you see any points of comparison with the conversation in the garden of Eden?
2 The Phantom states that the games they have played until then are at an end. What was the nature of these games?
3 There is some interesting fire imagery in this song. What do the characters do with it?
4 How do you react to the Phantom's singing Raoul's love song to Christine? How does Christine feel?
5 Compare the Phantom's controlling nature with that of a cult leader or a political tyrant. Is Jesus like this?

BIBLE QUOTES

Passionate love

(Also known as *eros*)
Now to the unmarried and the widows I say: it is good for them to stay unmarried, as I am. But if they cannot control themselves, they should marry, for it is better to marry than to burn (with passion).

(1 Corinthians 7:8-9)

True love

(Also known as *caritas,* or *agape*)
Love is patient, love is kind. It doesn't envy, it doesn't boast, it's not proud. It's not rude, it's not self-seeking, it's not easily angered, it keeps no record of wrongs. Love doesn't delight in evil but rejoices with the truth. It always protects, always trusts, always hopes, always perseveres.

(1 Cor 13:4-7)

©*iStockphoto/sirup*

By their fruit you shall know them

"Watch out for false prophets. They come to you in sheep's clothing, but inwardly they are ferocious wolves. By their fruit you will know them. Do people pick grapes from thorn bushes, or figs from thistles? Likewise every good tree bears good fruit, but a bad tree bears bad fruit. A good tree cannot bear bad fruit and a bad tree cannot bear good fruit. Every tree that does not bear good fruit is cut down and thrown into the fire. Thus, by their fruit you will know them."

(Matthew 7:15-20)

Chapter Six

Seeing in the Dark

Plot Summary: *Phantom of the Opera* (6)

Once again we see the Phantom punting Christine across the subterranean lake as the police and the mob pursue him. When they arrive in his murky lair Christine is shocked to see a dummy of herself crumpled on a throne, dressed in a wedding gown. Christine realizes at last that it is not just the Phantom's scarred face that has caused his misery and loneliness—his unhappiness stems also from his own use of violence and mercilessness as a solution *(it's in your soul that the true distortion lies)*.

Meanwhile Raoul has found his way to the lair, and he bravely faces the Phantom, begging him to let Christine go.

Song Summary

The Phantom's Lair

The Phantom calls his lair the dungeon of his black despair, where he is locked up in the prison of his mind. He tells Christine that part of his despair is caused by the fact that he was chained in that dark and dismal place, not for any mortal sin but for the wickedness of his abhorrent face. He asks her why nobody has ever showed him any compassion or uttered a kind word to him, but Christine can provide no answer. When they arrive at his lair, Christine is horrified by the dummy he has built in her likeness. She asks him if she is to be prey to his lust for flesh now that he has gorged his lust for blood. He explains that the fate which condemns him to wallow in blood has also denied him the joys of the flesh. He then removes the bridal veil from the dummy and puts it on Christine's head. She tells him that his haunted face holds no horror for her now, for it's in his soul that the true distortion lies.

Raoul climbs out of the water behind the portcullis and demands that the Phantom free Christine. He asks him to show pity, but the Phantom reminds him that the world never showed him any compassion at all.

Commentary

Beauty and the Beast

When the Phantom blames "the wickedness of his abhorrent face" for landing him, bound and chained, in this cold and dismal lair, we are reminded of the old theme of "Beauty and the Beast," which appears many times throughout literature and which also inspired the novel on which this musical is based. Here the Phantom/Beast is presented as a tragic figure, a man whose unfair and unfortunate fate has caused him to become hurt and embittered as a result of his horrible disfigurement. He is a lonely, brilliant, creative genius who yearns to be accepted for who he is on the inside. He needs Christine's love for his redemption and self-affirmation, and the reader tends to sympathize with his plight.

The Phantom as a demonic figure

In the musical, however, the Phantom seems to symbolize the dark side of the spiritual realm with which all humans struggle. During the auction that takes place in the opening scene of the musical, the Phantom is introduced with the number of the Beast in Revelation (666), and his murders and accidents are caused in a supernatural way. His character is egotistic and demanding (he must have free passes, his own special box, and the right to do all the casting), as well as possessive (he wants to "create" Christine according to his own lights) and choleric (he easily falls into rages when crossed). His love for Christine suggests Don Juan's desire for conquest, and it also brings to mind Pygmalion's wish to create Galatea as his own work of art.

The Phantom: Demonic or human?

The Phantom seems almost too demonic to be fully human, yet at the same time he seems too human to be completely convincing as a demonic figure. If he is indeed a profoundly misunderstood and unfortunate person, then he deserves our sympathy (tempered with discernment, of course). But if he is symbolic of the Devil himself, then he is claiming rights (the right to be loved, for example) that are not his.

Andrew Lloyd Weber chose to present the Phantom as a man who is too human to be "demonically correct," and this approach provides many good opportunities for discussion—especially after the last act of the musical.

Questions

1 Compare the Phantom with the Beast in "Beauty and the Beast."
2 The Phantom says he lives in darkness deep as hell. What do you think hell means in this context?

3 Does the Phantom deserve to live in a murky lair? Is this
   some kind of a punishment, or did he choose it?
4 Are we responsible for our own destinies, or should we
   blame our unhappiness on others?
5 Are we determined by our DNA? What about free will?
6 Discuss nature versus nurture.
7 Is life fair? How should we play the cards that are dealt
   to us? What does God want of us?

Chapter Seven

Farewell to the Fallen Idol

Plot Summary: *Phantom of the Opera* (7)

The Phantom seizes Raoul and strings him up in a noose which is suspended from thin air. He turns to Christine and gives her a choice: either she marries him and he lets Raoul go, or she refuses and he kills Raoul.

Christine kisses the Phantom on the lips while Raoul watches, horrified. The Phantom is as good as his word and releases Raoul. As the police and the mob approach, the Phantom suddenly tells Christine to escape in the boat with Raoul. Christine gives him back his ring, then flees with Raoul. The Phantom sits on his throne and watches them leave together.

Just as the police are about to seize him, he wraps his cloak around himself and then mysteriously disappears. All that is left is his mask...

Song Summary

The Final Threshold

With Raoul dangling from a rope in thin air, the Phantom is presented as both a human being and a supernatural figure as well. He gives Christine a choice: Start a new life with him and buy Raoul's freedom, or refuse him and send Raoul to his death. This, he adds, is the point of no return.

Christine is angered by this cruel choice, and tells him that the tears she might have shed for him have turned to tears of hate. She calls him a false friend and a fallen idol, but hesitates nonetheless. Raoul begs her not to throw her life away for his sake, but Christine sees the torment in the Phantom's heart and realizes that he is a "pitiful creature of darkness." She asks God to give her the courage to show him that he's not alone, and she kisses him tenderly, prompting the Phantom to cut Raoul down.

At this point the police and the mob appear on the scene, shouting angry epithets and with blood lust and revenge in their hearts. Christine realizes that the Phantom is like the rest of us—there is both good and evil in his soul. Good takes the upper hand, and the Phantom puts Christine first, instructing her to take the boat and flee with Raoul, who is in a better position to make her happy. As Christine hurries away, the Phantom calls out that he loves her.

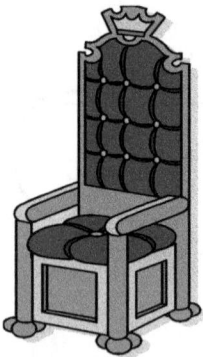

His heart breaks as he hears Christine sing a duet with Raoul in the boat, where they say to each other: *Share each day with me, each night, each morning.* The Phantom cries out that Christine alone can make his song take flight. "It's over now, the music of the night."

Commentary

The Phantom's epiphany: a kiss

It is Christine's warm kiss that prompts the Phantom to show mercy to her and to modify his hatred and jealousy of Raoul, sending the young lovers away to enjoy the rest of their lives together. This was the Phantom's moment of epiphany, when for the first time he was shown the love and mercy that he had always yearned for but had never known before. At that moment a new Phantom was born.

This symbolizes the basic doctrine of Christianity, which teaches that human beings are saved by God's grace through Jesus Christ, who laid down his life for us all. The moment of epiphany is that special time when one is born again as a new creation. We will see this happen in the case of Jean Valjean, too, when the Bishop of Digne gives him a silver candelabrum, a gift which causes him to become a totally new person when he experiences God's love for the first time. This will also occur in the next musical, when Don Quixote's love transforms Aldonza into a new creation by showing her how to see herself as she really is.

Whatever one's interpretation, the Phantom was a hurt and suffering human being, one who displayed more than the usual number of sins, but who, like other imperfect creatures, had his moments of beauty. Christine's kiss gave him a flash of light in a tragic life of darkness—a sudden ray of sunshine in the shadows.

We would do well to be careful not to thank God that he didn't make us like the Phantom, for we are all, in one sense or another, like the Phantom anyway, for better or for worse. We all wear masks to cover our faults and failures. We can only hope that we may be blessed with an epiphany of our own when we most need it—an epiphany given to us at the perfect moment as a special gift from a loving God.

Questions

1 Why do you think the Phantom allowed Christine to leave with Raoul?
2 Why did Andrew Lloyd Webber give the Phantom super-natural abilities?
3 In what ways is he a demonic figure, and in what ways is he all too human?
4 Should we allow ourselves to judge the Phantom? Do you think it's hard to practice discernment without judging?
5 Can the Phantom teach us anything about ourselves? Who among you would like to elaborate?
6 What does the name "Christine" mean? Does this have a bearing on the meaning of the Phantom's epiphany?
7 At the end of the musical, all that is left of the Phantom is his mask. What does this mean in terms of his epiphany?
8 Have you ever had an epiphany?

Definition of *epiphany*

1. An appearance or manifestation, especially of a deity.
2. A sudden intuitive perception of, or insight into, the reality or essential meaning of something, generally initiated by some simple, homely, or commonplace experience.
3. A literary work or section of a work presenting, usually symbolically, such a moment of revelation and insight.

Man of La Mancha

Etching by Gustave Doré

Transformational Love

Chapter Eight

The Nobility of the Age of Chivalry

Plot Summary: *Man of La Mancha (1)*

The curtain opens to reveal a dark dungeon where shadowy prisoners can be seen clanking their chains and muttering dark threats. Miguel de Cervantes (Spain's greatest prose writer, 1547-1616) has been arrested for running afoul of the Spanish Inquisition. The unsavory types (with whom he shares the dungeon) try to steal his meager possessions. To distract and placate them, Cervantes offers to entertain them with a tale he has written about an elderly gentleman who has read so many novels of chivalry that he has gone slightly dotty in the process. This deluded gentleman feels that he, like the brave knights of ancient times, must also sally forth onto the highways and byways of the nation and right all the wrongs he may encounter.

To accomplish this he marches off to the town dump and gathers some scraps of metal to make a suit of armor. He proclaims himself to be "Don Quixote de la Mancha" (the province of his birth), then he mounts a skinny old nag and sets forth in search of adventure.

It suddenly occurs to him that a real knight is always accompanied by a squire, so he persuades Sancho Panza, a rotund, down-to-earth peasant, to go with him. Unable to find another horse for Sancho, he provides him with a sturdy donkey instead.

> Filled with wild optimism and a profound sense of calling, Don Quixote and his trusty squire leave their village to present their services to widows, orphans, and damsels in distress, while fighting the heathens, wizards, and servants of sin who inhabit the "bleak and unbearable world" beyond the limits of their comfortable little town.

Song Summary

Man of La Mancha

In this introductory song, Don Quixote explains to his fellow prisoners that he will impersonate a knight errant facing a dangerous world with his banners all bravely unfurled. He will sally forth with his squire, Sancho Panza, who tells the audience that he'll proudly follow his master to the end. Don Quixote warns the evil men of his day that their dastardly doings are past, for he will see to it that virtue shall triumph at last.

Commentary

What's in a name?

Many people expecting a new baby will read long lists of names in order to find one that suggests a quality they would like their babies to have. Jesus also chose different names for a number of his disciples, changing Simon's name to Peter (meaning *the Rock)*, and referring to the *"Sons of Thunder"* when speaking of James and John (the sons of Zebedee). *(See Mark 3:16-17)*

Likewise Cervantes' country gentleman, whose real name was Alonso Quijana, struggled to come up with a name that might reflect his new identity. He ended up choosing "Don Quixote de La Mancha," believing it had a knightly ring to it.

Lifting up the humble

There is also considerable irony to be found in the sort of people whom God first chose for his own. They were a ragtag group of Hebrews living in an insignificant outpost of the Roman Empire. As for Jesus himself, he was from Galilee, the least important region of the outpost, and was the son of a modest, hard-working carpenter. He spoke Aramaic (the common language of his day) with a Galilean accent, which was just about as impressive to the Pharisees as a Cockney accent would be to a resident of Buckingham Palace.

Sancho Panza, too, must have spoken with a peasant's harsh accent that would have set a Spanish aristocrat's teeth on edge, and his last name, which means *"bread basket,"* is not an unsubtle description of his protruding belly.

Come, follow me

Jesus chose humble fishermen to be his followers, and they responded to his call with the straightforward enthusiasm of uncomplicated men. Don Quixote, too, invites a modest peasant (his neighbor from the village) to be his squire. Sancho agrees to follow him because he is moved not only by his master's lofty purposes, but also by the thought of escaping from his bossy, overbearing wife and by the hope of enriching himself with the spoils gained by defeating the evildoers of the world.

Mixed motives

Sancho's motives were just about as mixed as those of the disciples of Jesus, some of whom at first believed that they would be benefited in ways that would advance their political ambitions (overthrowing the Romans) and their personal glorification (sitting at the right hand of God in the new kingdom).

Don Quixote's quest

Be that as it may, Don Quixote himself has a clear vision of what he has been called to do, as we discovered from the opening stanzas of the musical. He yearns to be a Christian knight, marching forward with his banners unfurled, rescuing the weak and challenging the wicked with his trusty lance. But unfortunately his physical eyes do not always see things quite as clearly as do his spiritual eyes, for he constantly misunderstands the situations he encounters, with results that are uniformly both humorous and disastrous.

In one famous episode he mistakes a windmill for a dangerous giant, and he courageously attacks it. He suffers a humiliating defeat when he thrusts his lance into one of the sails of the windmill and is promptly yanked off his horse by the motion of the arm, which lifts him high into the air, then drops him unceremoniously onto the ground. The expression *"tilting at windmills"* has now come to refer to those fool-hardy individuals who assume that they can solve problems by precipitously throwing themselves into the fray without properly analyzing the situation or the likely outcome.

Questions

1 After hearing Don Quixote's "declaration of purpose" in the first song of *Man of La Mancha,* what are the motivating factors inspiring him to pursue his quest? From a Christian point of view, what (or who) has been left out of the picture? How might this affect the results?

2 Based on what you know of them so far, compare Don Quixote and Sancho.

3 What does your name mean? What would your motives be in naming a child? Do you think the disciple Peter was like a rock from the very beginning?

4 Can you name some humble characters in the Bible who achieved unexpected victories? Why do you think God chose apparently weak or flawed servants to carry out his purposes?

5 Why do you suppose Don Quixote chose an uneducated peasant to be his squire, a peasant who had never even heard of squires before? How does it compare to Jesus' motives in choosing humble fishermen to follow him?

6 Do you think some people may have mixed motives in becoming Christians?

7 Can you think of some examples of people who tilt at windmills? What were the results? What is the remedy?

Notable Quotes

"See to it, when you write your story, that those of melancholy temperament shall be moved to laughter, the sanguine shall laugh the more, those of few wits shall not be bored, intelligent readers shall admire the originality, those of grave temperament shall not scorn it, and the wise shall have reason to praise it."

—*Cervantes (advice given to the author by an imaginary friend, from the prologue of "Don Quijote de la Mancha")*

Chapter Nine

Don Quixote in Love

Plot Summary: *Man of La Mancha* (2)

After Don Quixote tilts at the windmill, knight and squire arrive, bruised and tired, at a roadside inn. Don Quixote takes one look at the inn and believes he has arrived at a castle. Meanwhile Aldonza (a servant girl and part-time prostitute) is being propositioned by a group of obnoxious mule drivers who happen to be staying there. She responds with a song describing them and herself in bitter terms.

When Don Quixote enters the "portals" of the inn he immediately falls in love with Aldonza, whom he mistakes for a princess. He calls her *"Dulcinea"(Sweet One,* loosely translated*),* and sings her a tremulous love song, but she understably assumes he is making cruel fun of her and will have nothing to do with the love-sick knight.

Song Summaries

It's All the Same

Aldonza sings to the audience, explaining that as far as she is concerned one pair of arms is like another, and when the lights are out no man burns with a special flame. She's nobody's fool, and is not taken in by promises of love. She tells the mule drivers to pay her well, and she'll give them what money buys.

Dulcinea

Don Quixote tells Dulcinea that he has dreamed of her all his life, and even though he has never seen her or touched her, he has known her with all of his heart. She has always been with him, he tells her, even though they have always been apart. He sees heaven when he gazes at her, and to him her name is like a prayer an angel whispers. The mule drivers immediately pick up on his song and repeat it back to him in mocking, sarcastic tones. The two interpretations provide a good example of the chiaroscuro of different human hearts.

Commentary

La belle dame sans merci

Now that Don Quixote has a squire to go with him on his quest, it occurs to him that all the knights he read about in the books of chivalry had ladies. Like the Muses of ancient times, these beautiful, elegant ladies provided inspiration for their men. If a knight slayed a dragon, it was for his lady. If he rescued an orphan or a damsel in distress, it was for her sake as well. Often she was demanding and hard to please, so the knight had to make sacrifices and endure hardship to win her favor. In fact, the crueler she was, the more deeply the knight would love and respect her. The French even had a name for this type of woman: *la belle dame sans merci* (the elegant lady without mercy).

Don Quixote, then, was on the look-out for a princess as he traveled the roads of Spain with his old friend, Sancho Panza. So eager was he to find the lady of his dreams that it's not surprising he mistook the servant girl at the inn for the ideal princess who occupied all his waking moments. Since Aldonza believed that Don Quixote was making fun of her, she reacted with a coldness that ranked her along with the other merciless but beautiful ladies of medieval tradition.

Mothers' advice

It wasn't long ago when mothers advised their daughters to play hard to get during courtship. *Be demanding,* they would say. *Keep him guessing. Don't wear your heart on your sleeve. Make him work for your favors. Don't give in.* This sort of motherly advice was a sure-fire recipe for turning out daughters who were well versed in the art of being a *belle dame sans merci.*

Women's liberation

Since the 1960's, however, women have taken on a totally different role, preferring equality in the boardroom and in the bedroom to the games their mothers taught them. Romance has suffered a blow as a result, but many modern women (and men, too) would say that romantic love was idiotic in the first place.

And yet... are we not still affected by the legacy of the romantics of yesterday? Why are men sometimes attracted to shrewish, abusive women? Why do we understand Carmen when she sings, *"You go for me, and I'm taboo, but if you're hard to get I go for you..."* Why do we still idealize ordinary folk, reach for forbidden fruit, or fall especially hard when there are separations and obstacles to deal with? Why do we say that *"absence makes the heart grow fonder"* (wouldn't it be easier to say, *"Out of sight, out of mind")?*

Mrs. Dulcinea

It is generally the prerogative of the young to mistake literature for life itself. We tend to go through "phases" when we yearn for a *grande passion.* The French seem to have a corner on the market when it comes to coining words to describe romance—it happens during youth, sometimes during a "middle age crisis," and occasionally in old age, when the hope of such an opportunity is all but lost.

But most of us already know that passionate love does not go well with the rather practical institution of marriage. It's hard to imagine a Mrs. Dulcinea Quixote bouncing a crying baby on her knee. We get over our romantic dreams, we lose our dependency on the Muses, we learn to live for others, and we wake up one morning only to discover, to our profound surprise, that we are happy after all.

Questions

1   It would appear that in the song called "It's all the Same," *aphros* has had a harmful effect on Aldonza. Explain.

2   In the song called "Dulcinea," Don Quixote's *eros* love irritates Aldonza even more than the coarse propositions of the mule drivers. Any comments?

3   Once again we have a situation where a name change has occurred. What are some of the contrasting characteristics that define Aldonza and Dulcinea?

4   Describe the *belle dame sans merci* and the effect she has on the men who love her. Why do her methods work in some circumstances?

5   Although our mothers' advice for a successful courtship was interesting, they didn't always stop advising us when we got married. What sort of advice did your mother give you for a successful marriage? What advice would you give a young person today?

6   Has the women's movement liberated us from romantic love? Is this good or bad? Both or neither?

7   Compare the Phantom's attempt to seduce Christine with Don Quixote's approach to courting Aldonza. Which one of the two men is initially more successful?

Chapter Ten

Trouble on the Home Front

Plot Summary: *Man of La Mancha* (3)

Back in Don Quixote's home town (even Cervantes himself has forgotten its name), his niece asks the local Padre what she can do to assist her mentally unstable uncle. The Padre agrees to go with her fiancé to bring her uncle home.

Meanwhile Don Quixote asks Sancho to deliver a love-note to his lady. Aldonza can't imagine what Sancho sees in the old gentleman, so she questions him at some length about why he follows him.

Song Summaries

I'm Only Thinking of Him

Don Quixote's niece is beside herself. Her uncle is now the laughing-stock of the village, but in spite of the humiliation his madness is bringing down upon her head, she is only concerned about his welfare. "In my body it's well known," she assures the Padre, "there is not a selfish bone." She's been told he's chasing dragons, and she fears it may be true. But what really worries her is that if her fiancé hears about it, heaven only knows what he might do. The old housekeeper pipes up and informs the Padre that she has heard he's seeking a lady to be his own true love, and she worries that in his madness he might choose *her*. Even if this turns out to be true, she says, she will grimly guard her honor while she continues to act only in his best interests. The Padre takes the audience into his confidence as he admits to us in ironic tones that he is deeply impressed with their saintly pleas and their kindness in thinking only of him. "What a comfort to be sure," he adds with a wink, "that their motives are so pure, as they go thinking and worrying about him!"

I Really Like Him

When Aldonza asks Sancho why he follows Don Quixote, he says it's essentially because he likes him. "But what do you get out of it?" Aldonza wants to know. Sancho can only repeat that he likes him, and that you can barbecue his nose, make a giblet of his toes, make him freeze, make him fry, make him sigh, make him cry, he'll still like him.

Commentary

Only the purest of motives

We can't help but smile at the hypocrisy of Don Quixote's niece when she asks the Padre to help her bring her uncle home again. Of course, she and the housekeeper assure him, they have only his best interests in mind. A gentleman of his advanced years would be much more comfortable at home (where he would no longer be able to subject them to public humiliation with his unorthodox behavior and quirky ideas).

But are we not all guilty of presenting ourselves in such a way as to make others think we are just a little better than we really are? I once knew a man who used to complain that the world was nothing but a vast desert of rampant mediocrity. We could just as easily substitute *"hypocrisy"* or *"self-interest"* for *"mediocrity,"* and we wouldn't be far from the truth. What can we say, then, when our friends tell us they don't want to visit our churches because there are so many hypocrites there?

Naturally we're not going to suggest that they examine the beams in their own eyes first, but it is true that Christians are often mistaken for people who believe they have a corner on the market when it comes to virtue (or perhaps some Christians like to give that impression). It would be a good idea for us to remind our friends, however, that churches are not clubs set up to honor the virtuous, but hospitals to help the sick. It would be just as incongruous to think of churches as gathering places for the "good" as it would be to imagine that hospitals are filled with patients claiming to be perfectly healthy (and maybe even a little healthier than other people).

Following the master

Sancho tells Aldonza more or less the same thing when she asks him why he follows Don Quixote. He likes him. He wants to be with him. He wants to walk the roads with him, and share adventures with him, and get to know him better. He can't quite figure out how to explain this to Aldonza. He only knows that he wants to spend all his time with the knight. Even though he can't always understand the details of his master's quest, the loyal squire accompanies him anyway, simply because he likes him. There's something about Don Quixote that attracts him, and he follows.

Questions

1 Have you ever had a mentor, friend, or loved-one whom you have admired greatly? What was she or he like?"
2 Why does Sancho follow Don Quixote? Would you be tempted to follow him, too? Do you see any similarities between Don Quixote and Jesus?
3 Why do you suppose the first disciples left their fishing behind and followed Jesus without a second thought?

Bible Quote

Following Jesus

Then he called the crowd to him along with the disciples and he said: "If anyone would come after me, he must deny himself and take up his cross and follow me. For whoever wants to save his life, will lose it, but whoever loses his life for me and for the gospel will save it. What good is it for a man to gain the whole world, yet forfeit his soul? Or what can a man give in exchange for his soul? If anyone is ashamed of me and my words, the Son of Man will be ashamed of him when he comes...

Mark 8:34-38

Cartoon ©Sonia Harrison Jones

He says he's going to make us fishers of men!

Chapter Eleven

Don Quixote Stands Vigil

Plot Summary: *Man of La Mancha* (4)

While Don Quixote is "standing vigil" in the courtyard of the inn, Aldonza approaches him and asks him why he does the things he does. But before he can find an answer for her an itinerant barber comes along, wearing his polished brass shaving basin on his head to protect himself from the sun. Don Quixote mistakes the shaving basin for "the golden helmet of Mambrino," a magic helmet worn by one of the great heroes of the novels of chivalry that Alonso Quijana loved so much. Don Quixote demands that the barber hand over the helmet, which he intends to wear in a special ceremony when the innkeeper dubs him a "knight."

Song Summaries

What Do You Want of Me?

Aldonza is completely baffled by Don Quixote, and doesn't mind telling him so. She wants to know why he marches through the dream that he's in, covered with glory and rusty old tin. Furthermore, she wants to know why he rushes at the world all alone, fighting mad battles that aren't his own. She asks him if he realizes that he's laughed at wherever he goes, and she confesses to him that she cannot laugh with the rest, but she doesn't know why. She begs him to tell her what he wants of her.

The Barber's Song

Along comes the barber, singing happily about how nicely he can earn his pay with his razor and his basin, for the Lord protects his barbers 'cause he makes the stubble grow. Don Quixote approaches him and demands that he hand it over. The barber tells him it's nothing but a shaving basin, but Don Quixote quickly disabuses him of that notion, and explains that it's the golden helmet of Mambrino, with a very illustrious past. The barber is quite sure he can hear the cuckoos singing in the cuckooberry tree. Sancho warns the barber that if his master says it's a helmet, he'd better agree.

Commentary

Responding to love

At this point in the musical, Aldonza seems to take a deeper interest in the old knight errant, who is convinced that she is a beautiful lady worthy of the deepest love and respect. She understands now that it isn't his intention to make fun of her, but she doesn't know what to make of his unorthodox view of the world. She realizes his quest is full of contradictions. On the one hand he wears nothing but a flimsy suit of armor made of rusty tin, yet at the same time he is brave, noble, compassionate, and undeterred by the many obstacles that confront him. He is not concerned by the fact that the whole world is laughing at him. He merely plunges forward, ready for battle, eager to right whatever wrongs he may encounter, seeing good everywhere he goes. Like a modern day Noah, he follows his impossible vision despite the jeering crowds.

This, ironically, is the sort of destiny that God calls us to when we hear his voice and follow him. If we imagine that being a Christian is going to provide us with social status and respectability, we are heading in the wrong direction. Both Jesus and Cervantes hated every form of self-righteousness and pomposity, especially the kind that existed in the minds of the Pharisees of ancient Israel and the Inquisitioners of Golden Age Spain. Christianity is nothing if it doesn't reflect a deep love of both God and his creatures, but there's little room for love in the hearts of the high and mighty.

Where does this leave Aldonza? She senses that Don Quixote's love is sincere, but how is she to respond? She can't imagine how he can be so blind to her "real" self—her true nature. Would he still love her if he could see her as she thinks she really is? Aldonza hesitates, unsure of what to do. What does he see in her? Why does he choose her? Is he completely deluded, or is he a man of unusual sensitivity and depth? Aldonza decides to adopt a "wait-and-see" attitude.

Fact and fantasy

We smile at Don Quixote's whimsical interpretation of the barber's basin, but his view of it is much more inspiring than our own. We see it as an ordinary object with no special significance, but to Don Quixote the illustrious shaving basin is imbued with magical powers that will help him succeed in his quest to win the glory to which he aspires.

The discovery of the basin comes at a time when the beleaguered knight errant is feeling very discouraged by the unsuccessful results of some of his recent adventures. He blames his failures on the interference of Merlin, an evil magician determined to bring his good works to naught. But the basin represents a supernatural force that will counteract Merlin's efforts, and Don Quixote seizes it with unparalleled delight.

The forces of good have manifested themselves at last, and there is no doubt in the knight's mind that they will help him prevail over the forces of evil. Don Quixote, wearing the Golden Helmet of Mambrino, will march forth into the world and accomplish great feats.

Heroic muddling

Don Quixote has now assembled all the pieces of a heroic adventure: he is impeded by the forces of evil (Merlin), assisted by the forces of good (Mambrino), and inspired by his love for his lady (Dulcinea). On a Christian level we are involved in a similar scenario: we are opposed by Satan and his demons, we are helped by God and his angels, and we are inspired by our love for Jesus.

As Christians we may not think our role in this adventure is as misguided or as humorous as that of Don Quixote, but we don't know how we look from God's point of view. We might be surprised to learn that we seem just as misguided and perhaps even more ridiculous to the Father who quietly observes us with a melancholy smile as we muddle our way through life.

Questions

1 Aldonza asks Don Quixote why he does the things that he does. Do you think the first witnesses of Jesus' mission were similarly puzzled?
2 Aldonza wonders what Don Quixote wants of her. What do you think Jesus wants of you?
3 Aldonza has difficulty responding to Don Quixote's love. Why are some of us troubled initially by Jesus' love?
4 Don Quixote's armor is complete now that he has found the Golden Helmet of Mambrino. Discuss the spiritual armor that we are called upon to wear on our journey.
5 Don Quixote believes his quest is being opposed by Merlin, but he is certain that Mambrino's helmet will help him to prevail. Discuss the Christian concept of spiritual warfare in this connection (see next page).
6 How do you think today's world looks from God's point of view?

Bible Quotes

Spiritual armor

Therefore put on the full armor of God, so that when the day of evil comes, you may be able to stand your ground... Stand firm then, with the belt of truth buckled around your waist, with the breastplate of righteousness in place, and with your feet fitted with the readiness that comes from the gospel of peace. In addition to all this, take up the shield of faith, with which you can extinguish all the flaming arrows of the evil one. Take the helmet of salvation and the sword of the Spirit, which is the word of God. And pray in the Spirit on all occasions with all kinds of prayers and requests. With this in mind, be alert and always keep on praying for all the saints.

—Ephesians 6:13-18

Bible Quotes

Spiritual warfare

Put on the full armor of God so that you can take your stand against the devil's schemes. For our struggle is not against flesh and blood, but against the rulers, against the authorities, against the powers of this dark world and against the spiritual forces of evil in all the heavenly realms.

—Ephesians 6: 10-12

Cartoon ©Sonia Harrison Jones

Aldonza begins to see Don Quixote in a new light.

Chapter Twelve

Don Quixote's Quest

Plot Summary: *Man of La Mancha* (5)

The Padre and the niece's fiancé try to bring Don Quixote home, but the knight refuses to abandon his quest. The two men put their heads together once again to see if they can figure out some other way to bring their friend to his senses. In the song entitled "To Each His Dulcinea," the Padre hopes that the cure will not prove to be worse than the disease.

Meanwhile, in an attempt to answer Aldonza's question about why he does the things he does, Don Quixote composes a credo and sings it to her in the now famous song called "The Impossible Dream."

Song Summaries

To Each His Dulcinea

The Padre faces the audience and sings a monologue, saying that we all need our Dulcineas... we need that secret hiding place where we can find the haunting face to light our secret flame. For with our Dulcineas beside us we can do most anything—outfly the bird upon the wing or hold moonlight in our hands. Yet, he warns us, if we build our lives on dreams it is prudent to recall that if we hold moonlight in our hands, we have nothing there at all. Yet, he adds wistfully, how lovely life would seem if we could only weave a dream to keep us from despair. He concludes that we all need our Dulcineas, even if she's only flame and air.

The Impossible Dream

At last Don Quixote manages to find the words to explain to Aldonza his purpose in life. His mission is to dream the impossible dream, to fight the unbeatable foe, to bear with unbearable sorrow, and to run where the brave dare not go. He yearns to right the unrightable wrong, to love pure and chaste from afar, to try, when his arms are too weary, to reach the unreachable star. His quest is to follow that star, no matter how hopeless or how far.

He goes on to tell Aldonza that he knows that if he can be true to this glorious quest, his heart will be peaceful and calm when he's laid to his rest. He proclaims that the world will be better for this, that one man, scorned and covered with scars, still strove, with his last ounce of courage, to reach the unreachable stars.

Commentary

Safe romance

Have you ever had the feeling that life is passing you by? Does it seem to you that everyone else is finding fulfillment in their jobs and in their marriages, while your life remains boring and utterly dreary? Surely you deserve a break today. What could be more exciting than a touch of romance? It would have to be safe romance, of course. You certainly wouldn't want to hurt anyone. But how could it possibly do any harm to dream about that handsome market analyst on the eleven o'clock news, or the striking young anchorwoman on channel 18? Their haunting faces might be just what you need to light your secret flame.

Better yet, how about cultivating a secret romance with someone on the internet? Then you could remain completely anonymous while you presented yourself to the other person as anyone you would like to be. And if that "secret someone" responds to you, you might discover the kind of romantic excitement that inspires you to accomplish great and noble things. Who knows, you might even outfly the bird upon the wing and hold moonlight in your hand!

The Padre agrees that life would seem lovely indeed if everyone could weave a dream to avoid sorrow and despair, but he is quick to remind us that those who hold moonlight in their hands have nothing there at all. People addicted to drugs, alcohol, or cyber-romance might feel their lives have been enhanced by such props, tools, and activities, but we all know they can't help us solve our problems or see us through the difficult times. They may provide moments of fleeting excitement or temporary inspiration, but they are just that—temporary. We yearn to enjoy lasting relationships in which we can give and receive *agape* love, but the opportunities elude us when we allow moonlight to become a lamp unto our feet.

The heavenly cause

Don Quixote's quest as described in *The Impossible Dream* resonates with us because it paints a dramatic picture of a life that is adventurous and heroic. It appeals to something deep inside our hearts that yearns for purpose, meaning, and lofty goals.

Many of us would like to dedicate ourselves body and soul to some worthy cause, and sometimes we do. We would like to clean up the environment, or campaign for a favorite politician, or improve the educational system of medical schools. But we also need to keep our feet on the ground. I remember an old joke that went something like this: "My wife and I share all the decisions. She decides what house to buy, what car to buy, what school to send the kids to, and how to raise them. I decide what should be done to erase famine in the Third World, and how to bring peace to the Middle East..."

Scan of a clay tile designed by a Puerto Rican artist called Sanremi, after the well-known sketch by Picasso

Perhaps when our goals become too lofty we lose track of the everyday responsibilities that require our attention, and sometimes, as in the case of Don Quixote, we run the risk of becoming the laughing stocks of the neighborhood. But when our goals are not lofty enough, we miss out on the sense of heroism and adventure that make life worthwhile.

In responding to Jesus' call to dedicate ourselves to his great commission, we might do well to recall Don Quixote's words when he talks about his impossible dream. We may smile at his misconceptions and at his often shaky grasp of reality, but how can we laugh at his determination to march into hell for a heavenly cause? Who can find it in his heart to laugh at the unstoppable knight who, scorned and covered with scars, still strives, with his last ounce of courage, to reach the unreachable stars?

Questions

1 Some people claim that God is an imaginary figure that people have created to keep themselves from despair. How can we respond to such a viewpoint?

2 Some say The Phantom of the Opera created Christine for his own purposes. How does he differ from Don Quixote, then, who also created Dulcinea? Compare the different outcomes.

3 Why do you think God created human beings?

4 Are your goals lofty enough? Is Don Quixote's quest too ambitious?

5 Where might we derive the strength and the inspiration to march into hell for a heavenly cause, and to strive, with our last ounce of courage, to reach the unreachable stars?

Notable Quote

Love is a state in which man sees things most widely different from what they are. The force of illusion reaches its zenith here as the sweetening and transfiguring power. When a man is in love he endures more than at other times; he submits to everything.

—Nietzsche, "The Antichrist," 1888

Cartoon ©Sonia Harrison Jones

"They say he seeks a lady who his own true love shall be. God forbid that in his madness he should ever think it's me!"

Chapter Thirteen

The Knight of the Woeful Countenance

Plot Summary: Man of La Mancha (6)

Aldonza sees the coarse, low-life mule drivers loafing in the courtyard of the inn, and they sing her a suggestive song ("Little Bird, Little Bird") as she passes by. Following the departure of the Padre and the niece's fiancé, Don Quixote defends Aldonza's honor in an unexpectedly successful battle with the oafish mule drivers. As a reward, the inn-keeper dubs him a knight and grants him a new name: the Knight of the Woeful Countenance.

Wanting to experiment with the idea of putting Don Quixote's idealism into practice, Aldonza tries to be kind to the mule drivers. They immediately interpret this overture to mean that she is giving them the "come on." They also blame her for having caused them to lose face during the infamous battle with Don Quixote, so they turn on her and rape her, figuring that she "had it coming." They sing "Little Bird, Little Bird" again in evil tones as they swagger off, leaving her bashed and battered on the floor.

Song Summaries

Little Bird, Little Bird

The muleteers play with Aldonza as cats would play with a mouse, taunting her and mauling her as they get ready to rape her 'neath the cinnamon tree where they once learned to love, until one moonless night they had to say goodbye. Now they're asking the little bird in the cinnamon tree to have pity on them and bring her back to them. They've waited too long without a song since Don Quixote has been wooing her away from them into a glorious new world of high ideals and noble aspirations.

The Dubbing

After dubbing Don Quixote the "Knight of the Woeful Countenance," the innkeeper sends him on his way, assuring him that he will remember him for the rest of his life, and everyone he challenges will quail at the sight of him. He thanks God he won't be there to see the drubbings he will get when he challenges the many villains he will encounter as he fights for the rights of the innocent and the downtrodden.

Commentary

The mule drivers

Leering and wolf-calls suggest not only an absurdly elevated sense of self-worth on the part of the perpetrator, but such misplaced superiority also reveals an attitude ranging from disrespect to out-and-out hostility toward the object of the leer. This kind of an attitude is, of course, the very opposite of love. Don Quixote would never have whistled or leered at his lady Dulcinea, and even Don Juan would have known better than to insult his intended prey.

Yet there does seem to be a strange dichotomy in the hearts of some males that makes them want to divide women into two categories. A "good" woman ideally has all the attributes of the industrious wife and help-meet described in Proverbs. She is the sort of woman one marries and who bears children. But there is another kind of woman who also appeals to certain men—she is the woman one takes as a mistress, or the prostitute one visits secretly in the dead of night. She is the forbidden fruit who can offer all the thrills and excitement that a housewife, almost by definition, can't provide.

What causes these men to view women in such a light? Some scholars have suggested that Marianism (the worship of the Virgin Mary) has led to the idealization of the wife-mother role, while others believe that the culture of the Arab conquerers had a deep-seated and long-lasting influence on their Spanish hosts. It is not within the purview of a short study like this to analyze the behavior of those passionate souls who put their wives and mothers on pedestals while at the same time seeking excitement outside their marriages. Suffice it to say that it was never God's will for us to idealize our fellow creatures (as in the case of Don Quixote), nor did he want us to treat them as objects (the way the mule drivers treated Aldonza).

Questions

1 Why do you think the innkeeper dubbed Don Quixote the "Knight of the Woeful Countenance?"

2 Compare with Jesus, who was described in the Bible as a *man of sorrows, and acquainted with grief.* Isaiah 53: 2-3

3 Do you think the mule drivers have a rather high opinion of themselves? What do you think motivates them to behave as they do?

4 What do the mule drivers, the Phantom of the Opera, Don Juan, and Don Quixote have in common?

Bible Quotes

A man of sorrows, and acquainted with grief:
He had no beauty or majesty to attract us to him, nothing in his appearance that we should desire him. He was despised and rejected by men, a man of sorrows, and acquainted with grief. Like one from whom men hide their faces he was despised, and we esteemed him not.

— Isaiah 53: 2-3

The wife of noble character:
A wife of noble character who can find? She is worth far more than rubies. Her husband has full confidence in her and lacks nothing of value. She brings him good, not harm, all the days of her life... Charm is deceptive, and beauty is fleeting: but a woman who fears the Lord is to be praised.

— Epilogue to the Proverbs

Hiding his word in our hearts:
How can a young man keep his way pure? By living according to your word. I seek you with all my heart; do not let me stray from your commands. I have hidden your word in my heart that I might not sin against you.

— Psalm 119: 9-11

Chapter Fourteen

Aldonza's Creed

Plot Summary: *Man of La Mancha* (7)

After her experience with the mule drivers, Aldonza is now totally disillusioned with Don Quixote's idealistic dreams, which have brought her only pain and anguish. She tells the knight in no uncertain terms that she wants nothing further to do with him.

When Aldonza finishes this distressing song, Don Quixote suddenly finds himself face to face with a strange new enemy who calls himself the Knight of the Mirrors. He challenges Don Quixote to combat, forcing him to look into the mirror of reality shining forth from his shield. Don Quixote sees reflected there a fool and a madman, and he falls to the floor of the stage, defeated and in despair.

To add insult to injury, the Knight of the Mirrors takes off his disguise and reveals himself to Don Quixote. He is not Merlin the Magician (a worthy enemy indeed) but just an ordinary man—his niece's fiancé.

Aldonza has witnessed the knight's pain, and she feels a deep sense of empathy and loss when the Padre and the fiancé escort him off the stage. She leaves the inn and sadly trails behind the friends and family members who take the elderly gentleman home.

Song Summary

Aldonza

Aldonza faces Don Quixote and tells him she is not his lady, nor any other kind of a lady. She claims she was spawned in a ditch by a mother who left her there, naked and cold and too hungry to cry. Aldonza never blamed her—she was sure she left hoping that she'd have the good sense to die. She adds that most young ladies can point to their fathers with maidenly pride, but her "father" was a whole regiment of soldiers passing through town.

She tells him to take the clouds from his eyes and see her as she really is. He has shown her the sky, she says, but what good is the sky to a creature like her? Of all the cruel devils who badger and batter her, he is the cruelest of all. She explains that his gentle insanities rob her of anger and give her despair. She can take the blows and abuse of the mule drivers and their like, but she can't bear his tenderness. She makes it very clear that she is not Dulcinea, she is only Aldonza, a woman who is no one and nothing at all.

Commentary

Who are we?

After reaching out to Don Quixote and attempting to put his idealism into practice, Aldonza's encounter with the mule drivers causes her to retreat into the safety of her customary self-image. She may have low self-esteem, but at least she knows (or thinks she knows) who she is, and she describes herself with startling clarity.

Aldonza's description of her harrowing past life falls on deaf ears. Don Quixote seems to understand nothing of what she recounts, and continues to see her as a "lady" in every sense of the word. Perhaps he is idealizing her, or perhaps he is seeing only what he wants to see. On the other hand, it is entirely possible that he has spiritual vision that allows him to appreciate the inner person and to discern the beauty of a troubled woman hardened by an impossibly cruel life.

At this point, however, Aldonza is only irritated, rather than touched, by his vision of her inner beauty. Perhaps she also feels threatened by the implications of a way of seeing the world that is so different from her own. What would the future hold for her if she were to move, even slightly, in Don Quixote's direction? How would the numerous and radical changes affect her life? How would she cope? How would she adjust? Who would she be? What would she become?

Seekers contemplating a commitment to the Christian walk reach a certain point when they ask themselves these questions, and the answers are not always easy to accept. Those of us who became Christians later in life also struggle with our new identity as we leave the old ways behind. There is often a period of time (before we "let go and let God") when we feel a bit schizophrenic. But God doesn't let go, even when, like Aldonza, we let out a frustrated scream.

Mirror, mirror on the wall

Don Quixote's battle with the Knight of the Mirrors is a turning point in the story. In the stage production there is a well-choreographed ballet sequence where several knights confront Don Quixote, so that no matter where he turns he sees his image in their polished shields. But what is the truth? Is Don Quixote really just a foolish old man who has lost touch with reality? Is Aldonza merely a prostitute?

The tragedy for Don Quixote is that he can't see himself in the same way as he sees the heart of his lady Dulcinea. When he gazes at his own image in the shields, he sees only a feeble, daft old man dressed in rusty tin, seeking glory in all the wrong places. When he looks at himself he sees just an ordinary exterior, whereas when he contemplates Aldonza he discerns the inner "lady" in much the same way as God sees us as we truly are. Don Quixote sees himself through a glass, darkly, but when he looks at his beloved Dulcinea, the scales seem to fall off his eyes.

Don Quixote's love, then, has its effect on Aldonza, who feels deeply troubled when she witnesses his defeat at the hands of the Knight of the Mirrors. But who in the entourage has faith in Don Quixote de la Mancha? Who shares the dream? Who believes in the quest? Sancho "likes" him and loyally follows him, but only until an authority figure shows up and tells him it's time to go home. As for Aldonza, she's on the threshold, but she hasn't yet achieved an epiphany and so cannot help the knight in his hour of need.

It's never wise to look too deeply into mirrors. Narcissus drowns in his own image, the Phantom gains unfair access to Christine's soul, Snow White's stepmother goes insane with jealousy, and Don Quixote, broken, tired, and thoroughly discouraged, abandons his heroic quest.

Questions

1   If your daughter were a server at Aldonza's inn, how would you advise her to deal with the mule drivers?

2   In what manner does Don Quixote react to Aldonza's description of herself? Do you think his view of her is too idyllic? Is her opinion of herself too harsh and cynical?

3   How would you describe Jesus's view of us?

4   Why is Aldonza at first irritated, rather than touched, by Don Quixote's view of her character?

5   Why is the battle with the Knight of the Mirrors a turning point in the musical? Why is Don Quixote defeated?

6   What would you say is Don Quixote's tragic flaw?

7   What effect does his love have on Aldonza?

8   What might happen when we look into a mirror? Can you think of any mythical or literary figure who had problems with mirrors?

Quotes from the Bible
and from the Heidelberg Catechism

Who are we? We are not our own...
[My only comfort in life and in death] is that I am not my own, but belong—body and soul, in life and in death—to my faithful Savior Jesus Christ.

—LORD'S DAY 1
Heidelberg Catechism

Through a glass, darkly
When I was a child, I talked like a child, I thought like a child, I reasoned like a child. When I became a man, I put childish ways behind me. Now we see but a poor reflection as in a mirror; then we shall see face to face. Now I know in part; then I shall know fully, even as I am fully known.

—Corinthians 13: 11-12

Notable Quotes

Mirrors should reflect a little bit before throwing back images.

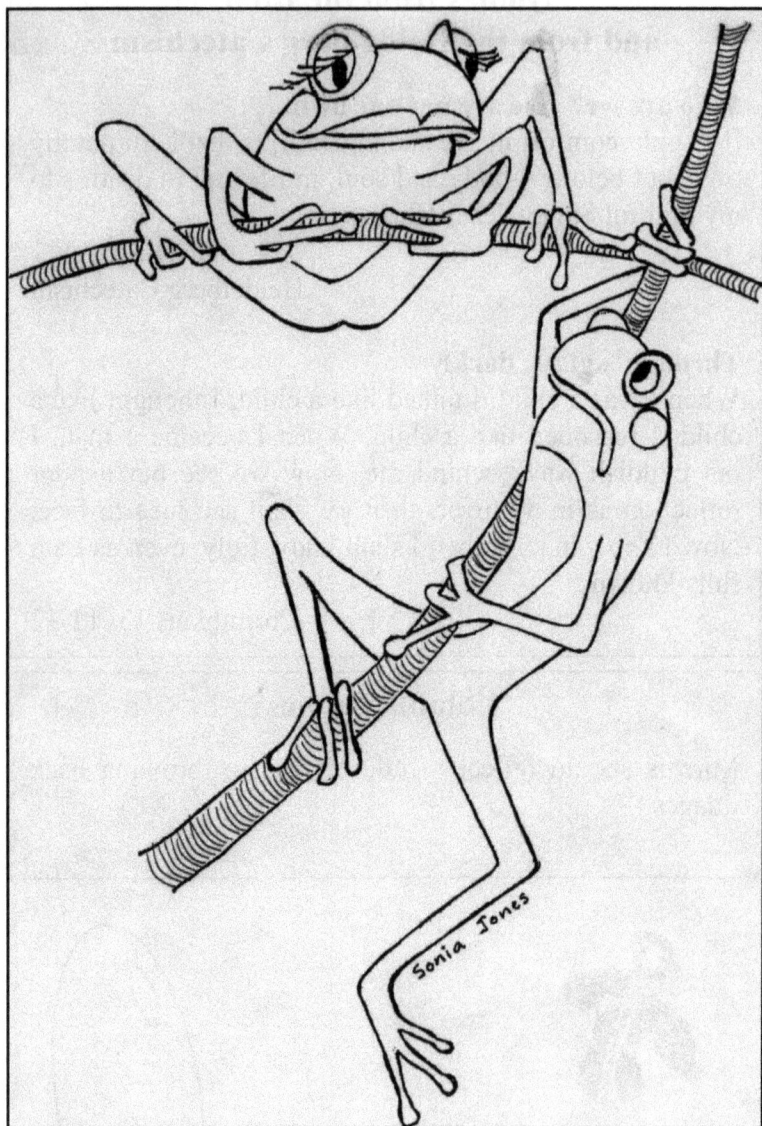

Cartoon ©Sonia Harrison Jones

But if you become a princess, where does that leave _me_?

Chapter Fifteen

Don Quixote lives!

Plot Summary: *Man of La Mancha* (8)

Alonso Quijana, the old gentleman who once called himself Don Quixote de la Mancha, is home again, languishing on his death bed. His neighbor, Sancho Panza, is by his side, trying his best to cheer him up with stories of local gossip. Aldonza, who has followed the group to Alonso Quijana's country house, is kneeling by his bedside, begging him to become Don Quixote again so he can restore the vision of glory he had shared with her such a short time ago. She poignantly urges him to remember that he called her by another name—*Dulcinea.*

As she helps him to recall the words of "The Quest," Don Quixote is suddenly inspired by his old memories and rises from his bed, calling for his sword and his armor so he can set out once more on his quest with his squire and his lady. But while he is singing the words to the "The Quest" in this moment of reaffirmation, he suddenly collapses on the floor. The Padre sings "The Psalm" over his lifeless body, but Aldonza refuses to accept the fact that he is dead.

"*Alonso Quijana* died," she says. "He seemed like a good man, yet I didn't know him. But *Don Quixote* is not dead," she declares. When Sancho Panza addresses her as Aldonza, she tells him that her real name is not "Aldonza," but "Dulcinea." Don Quixote, having recognized her all along as an individual of unique worth and value, has changed her forever by the strength of his love for her.

A Little Gossip

As Don Quixote languishes on his death bed, Sancho tries to restore his will to live by telling him all about the gossip in their village. He describes how his wife Teresa hit him, but had lost the knack of beating him properly. He hit her back, but she was made of harder stuff than he was. He reminds his master that whether the stone hits the pitcher or the pitcher hits the stone, it's going to be hard on the pitcher. His life is boring now that they're no longer on the road together. He hasn't fought a windmill in a fortnight, and a fiery dragon even visited him in his sleep, begging him to come out and play.

Dulcinea

Aldonza joins Sancho next to Alonso Quijana's bedside, and begs him to remember that he once found an unhappy girl and called her "Dulcinea." She pleads with him to wake up and bring back the bright and shining glory of Dulcinea.

The Impossible Dream

Quijana does indeed wake up, and asks Aldonza to remind him about the dream they lived together once upon a time. She tells him all about the quest, and about the impossible dream that inspired him to fight the unbeatable foe, and bear the unbearable sorrow, and run where the brave dare not go. Don Quixote picks up where she leaves off, speaking about righting the unrightable wrong, and loving pure and chaste from afar, and trying, when his arms are too weary, to reach the unreachable star…

Man of la Mancha

The final reprise of the musical's best songs continues as Aldonza falls to her knees in joy and gratitude while Don Quixote rises to his feet, shouting "Woe to the wicked!" as he asks for his armor and his sword. He hears the trumpets of glory calling him to ride, with his squire and his lady by his side. He manages to rise up from his death bed as he sings "I am I, Don Quixote, the Lord of La Mancha, our destiny calls and we go. And the wild winds of fortune shall carry us onward, whithersoever they blow... then he collapses and dies.

The Psalm and the Finale

The Padre sings "De Profundis clamavi [ad te], Domine" (*From the depths I have cried out to you, oh Lord,* from the Latin version of Psalm 130: 1-2), an echo of the psalmist's final cry and the most frequent prayer spoken at death beds ever after. All those gathered around him sing another finale of *The Impossible Dream.* The curtain falls on a beautiful musical based on one of the greatest masterpieces of world literature.

Commentary

Aldonza's epiphany: a new name

When Aldonza stands by Don Quixote's bedside pleading with him not to die, she reminds him that he once called her by another name. *Dulcinea* was the special name he chose for her, and when he spoke that name the very angels seemed to whisper it too. But now that Don Quixote has abandoned his quest, nobody calls her *Dulcinea.* She is Aldonza once again, and with the loss of her new name comes the absence of the special identity given to her by Don Quixote.

People have been sensitive to the importance of names since the beginning of time. God honored Adam when he asked him to name the animals; Plato talks about the importance of names in his *Dialogues;* Japanese artists take a new name when they attain higher levels in their art. In the New

Testament we're told to learn the names of the demons in order to have power over them. Even today, we often hear people say that they want to live up to their names.

And so it is that Aldonza refuses to accept the fact that Don Quixote has died. Alonso Quijana is dead, yes, but Don Quixote, his alter ego with the impossible dream, is still very much alive.

Aldonza, like Jean Valjean, has had an epiphany that changes her life. She understands now that Aldonza no longer exists. She has been born again as Dulcinea, and from now on she will be a new person. The bitter, cynical Aldonza has been transformed into Dulcinea, a new woman created by Don Quixote's love and respect. She is ready now to live her master's impossible dream, knowing that the wild winds of fortune shall carry her onward, whithersoever they blow.

The old, old story

This is another deeply moving version of the old, old story as far as Christians are concerned. We are called to become new creations in Christ (2Cor 5:17), and we are also invited to become fools for the Lord (1Cor 4:10). What we believe seemed like foolishness to the rational minds of the Greeks (1Cor 1:23) and to present-day skeptics as well, but our brand-new identities give us the kind of joy that Aldonza experiences after she becomes Dulcinea. We, too, hear the trumpets call and we march onward by our Master's side, carried forward by the gentle breeze of the Spirit.

Questions

1 Define the word "epiphany".
2 What does your name mean? Do you try to live up to it?
3 Does your perception of who you are change when you see yourself through the eyes of the person you love?
4 How does Aldonza's perception of herself change?

5 Why does the Christian faith seem like "foolishness" to
   the Greeks?
6 What sort of new creations do we become in Christ?

Foolishness to the Greeks

[20] Where is the wise person? Where is the teacher of the law? Where is the philosopher of this age? Has not God made foolish the wisdom of the world? [21] For since in the wisdom of God the world through its wisdom did not know him, God was pleased through the foolishness of what was preached to save those who believe. [22] Jews demand signs and Greeks look for wisdom, [23] but we preach Christ crucified: a stumbling block to Jews and foolishness to Gentiles, [24] but to those whom God has called, both Jews and Greeks, Christ is the power of God and the wisdom of God. [25] For the foolishness of God is wiser than human wisdom, and the weakness of God is stronger than human strength.

—1 Corinthians 1:20-25

New Creations in Christ

Therefore, if anyone is in Christ, he is a new creation: the old has gone, the new has come! All this is from God, who reconciled us to himself through Christ... We are therefore Christ's ambassadors, as though God were making his appeal through us.

—2 Corinthians 17-20

Les Misérables

Etching by Gustave Brion

Love and Redemption

Chapter Sixteen

From Convict to Mayor

Plot Summary: *Les Misérables* (1)

Down and out in Digne

Jean Valjean, a starving convict on parole, is roaming the streets of the town of Digne, looking for work. He has just finished serving nineteen years in jail for attempting several prison breaks after his original conviction for stealing a loaf of bread. The law requires him to display his convict's I.D. when he applies for work, so he is unable to find a job. As he sits on a curb—sick, shivering and close to despair—the Bishop of Digne invites him into his house for dinner and a good night's rest. Valjean is grateful for the hot meal and warm duvet, but he can't resist stealing the silverware while the Bishop is sleeping.

Some hours later Valjean is captured by Javert, a police officer and principle antagonist of the musical (the same man who threw Valjean into jail years before). He drags him back to the Bishop's house and invites the cleric to press charges so he can throw Valjean back into prison. But the Bishop insists that the silverware that Javert found on Valjean's person was his gift to the starving man. What is more, the Bishop points out to Valjean that he forgot to take the candelabrum he had given him. Javert, frustrated and angry, is forced to let Valjean go, but he vows to follow him to the ends of the earth to see to it that he is jailed once again.

Valjean's epiphany: the candelabrum

Jean Valjean is so deeply moved by the Bishop's kindness in telling Inspector Javert that he had given the silverware to Valjean as a gift that he, like the Phantom and Aldonza, has a sudden epiphany that causes him to undergo a life-changing experience. He is inspired to work hard and do his best to improve his circumstances, and within eight years he becomes a factory owner and the mayor of the town where he now lives (Montreuil-sur-Mer).

Valjean entrusts the management of his factory to a detestable foreman who is cunning enough to hide his cruel treatment of the workers from Valjean, whose duties as mayor prevent him from overseeing the man properly. The workers must put up with the foreman's abuse, for they know they will never find jobs elsewhere due to the high unemployment rate in the years following the French Revolution. The workers bemoan their fate in the next song.

The silver candelabrum that changed Jean Valjean's life

Song Summary

At the End of the Day

Although the women who work in Jean Valjean's factory are treated very badly by the lewd foreman, they have children at home who depend on them so they can't afford to quit their jobs or turn down the customers who demand sexual favors. Fantine, a lovely young factory worker, attracts the envy and spite of her co-workers, who rip off her necklace so they can sell it.

Jean Valjean hears the noise and comes to investigate. He tells them all to settle down, for he runs a business of repute, not a circus. When he leaves, the foreman asks them how the fight began. The women complain that Fantine has a daughter out of wedlock and has to pay a couple to take care of her while she is working. They claim she gets the money sleeping around, so at the end of the day she'll be nothing but trouble. They'll all end up in the gutter because of her. They tell the foreman she laughs at him while she's having her men, so he fires her in a fit of vindictive anger.

Commentary

Poverty and misery in Paris

As far as the poor in France were concerned, one of the most disappointing results of the Great Revolution of 1789 was its failure to live up to its famous motto of "Liberté, Egalité, Fraternité." During the aftermath of the revolution Charles X saw to it that the aristocrats, the clergy, and the bourgeoisie benefited greatly from the new order, but the working classes remained poor. Bitterness and cynicism continued to grow.

The attitudes expressed by the workers in Jean Valjean's factory no doubt reflected those of the impoverished working classes in France in the decades following the Revolution. By the 1820s and 1830s, many of the aristocrats who had fled the guillotine eventually returned to their homeland, where they enjoyed special privileges under the new king.

The poor were left scratching their heads. Many of them had died for the promise of freedom, equality, and brother-hood, but to what end? Why were they all still hungry and downtrodden? Why had they not even been granted the right to vote? How long would they have to be *les misérables* in a country where they were largely ignored by the ruling class?

God's spirit in everyday life

Victor Hugo, the author of the 19th-century masterpiece on which this musical is based, was too great a novelist to paint a uniformly bleak picture of the times. Although some of the clergy basked in their own wealth and influence, others were eager to use their material blessings for the benefit of the less fortunate. As we have seen, the Bishop of Digne's kindness and generosity of spirit had such a profound effect on Jean Valjean that his life was changed forever. From the moment he received the gift of the candelabrum, he saw himself not as a despised jailbird but as the creation of a loving God. He decided then and there to assume a leadership role in a small community that desperately needed a mayor who could come to the aid of the people and dole out justice at a time when the central government seemed unwilling or unable to do so.

Unacceptable conditions

As we mentioned before, Valjean's dual role as mayor and factory owner makes it difficult for him to attend to the well-being of his employees. Moreover, since unemployment was rife at the time, laborers found themselves at the mercy of managers who had the power to fire them whenever they felt like it. There were very few laws to protect the rights of the workers, so managers often allowed their power to go to their heads. They abused the laborers mercilessly, creating an atmosphere of tension and insecurity. This, in turn, led the workers to fight with one another for better positions in the pecking order. Poverty, abuse of power, and government neglect were all taking their toll on *les misérables*.

A fallen world

In circumstances such as these, human nature often reveals itself both at its worst and at its best. From the moment the curtain rises on the cold, dark panoramas of 19th-century France, we see illustrations of kindness and cruelty, of mercy and greed. The Bishop of Digne reflects God's uplifting spirit in his treatment of Jean Valjean, and the convict later mirrors this same spirit in his own attitude toward others.

The factory foreman, on the other hand, is the perfect example of self-seeking cruelty as he threatens his workers and insults them with his wandering hands. One sometimes wonders where God is hiding while this suffering is taking place. Why do bad things happen to innocent people?

Questions

1   After suffering so much injustice in his life, Valjean had every reason to be cynical. Yet his visit with the Bishop of Digne led him to believe in a loving, merciful God. How did this come about? What does this teach us?

2   How did Jean Valjean's conversion change his life? What effect did this have on other people in the musical?

3   *At the End of the Day:* The poor people described in this song also suffer (*"the righteous hurry past, they don't hear the little ones crying"*), yet we have seen that they themselves behave in a way that is heartless and cruel. Why do you think that is?

4   Why does the foreman pick on Fantine? Why do her
    fellow workers dislike her, too?
5   How do you think the Jewish traveler felt about the Good
    Samaritan? Do you think his life might have been trans-
    formed by the treatment he received?
6   Some people in this world have become street savvy and
    have learned to take advantage of kind people. Do you
    know of any examples of this? How should one react?

Bible Quote

One day an expert in religious law stood up to test Jesus
by asking him this question: "Teacher, what must I do to
receive eternal life?"

Jesus replied, "What does the law of Moses say?
How do you read it?"

The man answered, "You must love the Lord your
God with all your heart, with all your soul, with all your
strength, and with all your mind. And love your neighbor
as yourself."

"That is true," Jesus told him. "Do this and you will
live."

—Luke 10: 25-29

Chapter Seventeen

Fantine's Death

Plot Summary: *Les Misérables* (2)

After she loses her job, Fantine is forced to sell her locket, her hair, some of her teeth, and finally her body as well. She turns down a distasteful would-be customer who then tries to get back at her by falsely accusing her of cheating him. The legalistic, rigid Javert believes the loathsome man's accusation and is just about to drag Fantine off to prison when Valjean arrives on the scene and demands that she be taken to a hospital instead.

Later that day Javert sees Valjean rescue a man who is pinned down by a runaway cart. He is reminded of the amazing strength of convict 24601, and suspects that the mayor is that same man. From then on Javert pursues him relentlessly for the rest of the musical, wanting more than ever to jail him for breaking his parole.

Song Summaries

I Dreamed a Dream

In this lyrical song, Fantine explains how she fell in love one summer with a young man who then abandoned her when he grew tired of her. She is forced to leave her daughter Cosette in the care of the obnoxious Thénardiers while she works to support her.

Lovely Ladies

A crowd of wretched, poverty-stricken women are taunted by leering sailors who declare that they're hungry for a poke. Even the children are tough and cynical, as they have been witnesses to all the deplorable activities that take place every night on the pier.

Who Am I?

Jean Valjean finds himself in a desperate situation as well. Inspector Javert has been hunting him ever since he was released from prison, for he is convinced that Valjean the Convict will never become an honest man. He cleverly tells Valjean the Mayor that he has now caught the infamous ex-convict 24601 and has thrown him back into prison. Valjean can't bear the thought of an innocent man suffering in his place, so he admits to Javert that he is the actual convict he seeks. He confesses this in court so that the innocent man (invented by Javert) doesn't end up in jail.

Come to Me

After the court proceedings Valjean escapes once again so he can visit Fantine in the hospital. As Frantine lies dying—a victim of disease, poverty, hunger, injustice, cruelty and disillusionment—she begs Valjean to tell little Cosette she's sleeping and she'll see her when she wakes. He tells Fantine to be at peace, for he will always take good care of Cosette. She will want for nothing and nobody will harm her as long as he is living. Fantine dies, happy to know that Cosette will be in good hands.

Commentary

The question of free will

People often wonder how a good God can let bad things happen to his children. Why must life kill the dreams of a beautiful young woman? Why should a hungry, desperate man have his jail sentence extended nineteen years for trying to break out of prison on several occasions after being locked up there for stealing a loaf of bread? Why must a little girl be mistreated by cruel, cold-hearted people while her mother lies dying? Why is the world populated by *"les misérables"*? Surely this cannot be the will of a just and loving God.

And indeed it isn't. Let's go back to Eden for a moment and take a look again at how it all began. Many thoughtful people wonder why God put the forbidden fruit in the garden in the first place. If that tree hadn't been there, they say, our first parents could not have sinned, and human history would have been a joyful saga of never-ending love.

But if people *cannot* sin, do they have free will? And if they lack free will, can they love? A human being without free will would be something like a robot, dutifully obeying whatever his programmer instructed him to do. But God had higher plans for the humans he created. He wanted to love us and be loved by us in return, and he wanted us to experience the incomparable joy of sharing his delight in the universe he created. Nothing less than that would do.

When love becomes license

But free will, essential as it is to being fully human, also has some serious drawbacks. When one is granted the freedom to love deeply, one can also pervert that freedom into a license to love oneself above all others. That's exactly what Eve did. She believed the "serpent" (Satan in the form of a wily, devious creature of some kind*) when he promised her that if she ate the forbidden fruit she would be like God, knowing all things and enjoying eternal life. Christine was seduced by the Phantom in much the same way—he told her that if she followed him she'd "live as she had never lived before."

Temptation takes root

All temptation is similar in this respect. We are led to believe we're missing something enjoyable, so we begin to suspect that God has held back some of the pleasurable things in life. We doubt the goodness of God. Our love begins to dwindle. We are ungrateful for our blessings, we become dissatisfied with our dull lives, and we seek new alternatives. We need excitement. We want to live as we've never lived before so, like the Prodigal Son, we set off for the far country, while our father, with a breaking heart, waits patiently for us to come to our senses and return home.

What happens when the Prodigal Son leaves home and goes to that distant country? At first he is as happy as Pinocchio in Toy Land, but his excitement is short-lived. He soon learns that life outside his father's home is not what he expected. Yet in spite of his disappointment, it doesn't occur to him to blame his father for the poor conditions and the injustices of city living, and the father is not prepared, either,

* *Nobody knows what the serpent looked like when he spoke to Eve in the Garden of Eden. God changed him into a snake only after the Fall as a punishment for tempting Eve, so don't be fooled by all those paintings of a serpent coiled around an apple tree.*

to go to the city to protect the boy from every pickpocket or drug dealer. The city is what it is, and the son knows he chose to live there.

Who is to blame?

Ah, but *we* didn't choose to live in a world of suffering and tragedy! Why should *we* have to pay for the sins and foolish choices of Adam and Eve, the Prodigal Son, and other folks who existed before we were even born? *We* weren't in the Garden, and even if we had been, *we* wouldn't have eaten the forbidden fruit. We would have shown our love for God by trusting him and obeying his wishes.

Say no more! You have been granted the opportunity to exercise your free will too. You've been given a chance to show your love for God by following his Son who died so that you could be with him forever in the heavenly garden, where he has prepared a place for you.

We live in a world that is greatly influenced by the liar who deceived our first parents. If we're not happy to be here we would do well to remember that God has shown us the way to go home. Let's not forget to bring a candelabrum to light the way for others.

Questions

1 *I Dreamed a Dream:* Take a look at Fantine's dreams. Discuss how and why those dreams were crushed. What is your response to her misery?

2 *Who Am I?:* Valjean asks himself some specific questions about who he is. Discuss the definitions that he comes up with. How and why has he changed?

3 *Come to Me:* Fantine dies with a broken spirit, but she has hope for her child, Cosette. What's the basis for her hope?

4 If God is all-powerful, why does he let bad things happen
   to good people? Why does it seem he's not answering our
   prayers? Can he really care about our happiness when he
   allows a beloved spouse or a precious child to die?
5 Why did God allow the serpent to persuade Eve to eat the
   forbidden fruit?
6 Do you think it's an exaggeration to say we're *all* sinners,
   every one of us? Some of us, after all, have never been to
   jail or committed any crimes. If indeed we are all sinners,
   isn't the bar just a little bit too high?

Notable Quote

God created things which had free will. That means
creatures which can go either wrong or right. Some people
think they can imagine a creature that was free but had no
possibility of going wrong; I cannot. If a thing is free to be
good it is also free to be bad. And free will is what has
made evil possible. Why, then, did God give them free will?
Because free will, though it makes evil possible, is also the
only thing that makes possible any love or goodness or joy
worth having."

C.S. Lewis, "Mere Christianity"

Chapter Eighteen

Valjean Ransoms Cosette

Plot Summary: *Les Misérables* (3)

Just as Jean Valjean is closing the eyes of the deceased Fantine, Javert bursts into the hospital room and tries to arrest him. But Valjean, who is by far the stronger man, wrests himself free and explains to Javert that he must first ransom a little girl who is in the hands of two abusive innkeepers. He promises that once he rescues Cosette he will come back and turn himself in.

Javert doesn't believe him at all, nor is he interested in the ex-convict's agenda, so Valjean simply pushes him aside and escapes. He makes his way to the disreputable inn owned by the Thénardiers, and finds the five-year-old Cosette dressed in rags and feeling frightened because she has been ordered to venture out into the night to bring back a bucket of water from the well. She tries to keep up her spirits by imagining a better life.

Valjean is forced to linger a while at the Thénardier's inn before he manages to negotiate a ransom for the child. Once the exorbitant payment has been made to the venal couple, Valjean gathers Cosette into his arms and takes her away. He installs her in some rooms he has rented in Paris, and the two look forward to a good life together.

Summary of Songs

Confrontation

During the confrontation between Valjean and Javert in the dying Fantine's hospital room, Valjean asks the determined police inspector to show some mercy toward Fantine's child, whom he wishes to adopt. But Javert turns down his request, saying that a man like him can never change. Valjean tells him that he has more than paid his debt to society for the crime of stealing a loaf of bread and trying to escape from jail. He warns Javert that he is stronger than he is, and he has not yet run the race (see 1 Cor 9: 24-27), but Javert says he must think him mad to let him go after hunting him across the years. He reminds him once again that men like him can never change. Besides, his duty is to the law, and he will see that justice is done.

Castle on a Cloud

Fantine's little daughter, Cosette, dreams of living in a castle on a cloud where there are rooms full of toys and no floors for her to sweep. There are a hundred boys and girls for her to play with, and nobody shouts or talks too loud. There is a lady dressed in white who holds her and sings a lullaby and says, "Cosette, I love you very much." Nobody is lost, and nobody ever cries. A utopia indeed, for a sweet little girl.

Master of the House

Meet the totally repellent Thénardier, the self-described best innkeeper in town—not like those other crooks who rook the guests and cook the books. "Seldom do you see honest men like me," he tells the audience, "ready with a handshake and an open palm." He tells a saucy tale, makes a little stir, for customers appreciate a bon viveur. He doesn't mind confessing that he waters down the wine and steals the customers' knick-knacks when they can't see straight. Yes, everybody loves a landlord, but he'll be sure to skin you to the bone. He serves kidney of a horse, liver of a cat, and fills up all the sausages with this and that. He charges for the lice, extra for the mice, and two percent for looking in the mirror twice. In sum, he's a philosopher, companion, and a life-long mate, but his wife in no way shares his good opinion of himself.

The Thénardier Waltz of Treachery

When Valjean arrives at the Thénardier's place of residence to negotiate the necessary terms for relieving them of little Cosette, everybody's favorite landlord suddenly turns dewy-eyed and sentimental about his undying love for the child. "What a gem," he says. "What a pearl! Beyond rubies is our little girl! Let's not haggle for darling Cosette!"

Valjean offers him a fair price to cover their expenses (even though they never paid Cosette for her drudgery), and he takes her away with him to seek friendlier skies.

Commentary

Grace and the law

When God gave Moses the Ten Commandments, he spelled out for his people a list of do's and don'ts that showed them how to behave. God knew that if his wandering children loved him, this kind of behavior would come naturally. But they had only recently been liberated from Pharaoh's yoke, so God provided them with this extra guidance to get them through the desert—not only the physical desert but the spiritual desert as well. The commandments were a bit like a roadmap that was meant to help them see more clearly the way home.

But there is some danger in reading spiritual roadmaps as though they were physical ones—we run the risk of taking them too literally. We end up trying to stick to the letter of the law instead of following its underlying spirit. We ask questions like, "Does *not* working on the Sabbath include not turning on a light switch?" Then we go on to say, "If so, may I have someone else turn on the light switch for me?" We ask questions like these when we forget who God is and how to love him. Yet God himself never forgets how to love *us*, even when we disappoint him. When his laws failed to keep his people on track, God sent his only begotten Son to live among us and eventually die so that we could be forgiven for having eyes that don't want to see, ears that refuse to hear, and hearts that often seem incapable of loving.

Victor Hugo created a fine example of literal-minded legalism in Javert, the rigid, insensitive, self-congratulatory policeman who put the law above every other consideration. In contrast to Javert, Jean Valjean is transformed by the grace shown to him by God through the Bishop of Digne. His heart overflows with gratitude and love as he dedicates himself to helping others. The faithful ex-convict is a great example of what it means to live in God's mercy rather than under his law (no matter how brilliant we are at memorizing or interpreting that law).

Questions

1 *"Confrontation":* Describe and compare the two different types of chains that Valjean has worn in his life. What do these chains say to us?
2 Javert claims that men like Valjean can never change. Do you agree? What do Christians say about being born again and becoming new creations in Christ? How do the epiphanies in the musicals help you to understand this concept?

3 *"Castle on a Cloud"*: Cosette distracts herself from her misery by dreaming about a better place. Some people think that the Christian concept of heaven is a bit like "pie in the sky." What can one say to a bitter or dis-illusioned person who has come to believe that God is no more than an adult version of Santa Claus?

4 *"Master of the House"*: Even though there are some humorous lines in this song, many of the comments are crude and saddening in their blatant cynicism. Discuss how people can become jaded, and where this leads.

5 *"The Thénardier Waltz of Treachery"*: Calculating op-portunists such as the Thénardiers seem to flourish when there is social unrest. Discuss how bad times can bring out both the best and the worst in people. Give examples from present-day trouble spots.

6 What do you think of Valjean's negotiating skills?

7 How did Valjean finally succeed in wresting Cosette away from the Thénardiers?

Notable Quotes

On seeking the fresh approach:

People grind and grind away in the mill of a truism, and nothing comes out but what was put in. But the moment they desert the tradition for a spontaneous thought, then poetry, wit, hope, virtue, learning, anecdote, all flock to their aid.

—Ralph Waldo Emerson
Literary Ethics, 1838

©*iStockphoto/beakraus*

The Lord sets prisoners free...

Bible Quotes

Setting the Prisoners Free

He upholds the cause of the oppressed
and gives food to the hungry.
    The Lord sets prisoners free,
the Lord gives sight to the blind,
the Lord lifts up those who are bowed down,
the Lord loves the righteous.
    The Lord watches over the foreigner
    and sustains the fatherless and the widow,
but he frustrates the ways of the wicked.

Psalm 146: 7-9

Chapter Nineteen

The Insurrection

Plot Summary: *Les Misérables* (4)

Nine years have passed. The rabble and the students in Paris are very unsettled because General Lamarque, the only man in the government who ever took an interest in them, is about to die. Young Gavroche, a street urchin, hangs around the people as they bicker among themselves and complain about their plight *("Look Down")*.

Javert is in Paris too, still hot on the trail of Jean Valjean and determined to put him back in jail *("Stars")*. Their paths cross when he rescues Valjean and Cosette from an attack by a street gang led by the Thénardiers, but he doesn't recognize his old nemesis until after he has disappeared. Javert thinks of himself as being a righteous man whose duty is to see justice done. He is convinced that his view of Valjean as an untrustworthy criminal is the correct one. He does not believe in redemption for the average sinner or criminal—salvation is reserved only for good, law-abiding citizens like himself.

Meanwhile Valjean and Cosette (who has grown into a beautiful young woman) are going home when Cosette happens to meet the student, Marius. It is love at first sight, but neither one knows how to contact the other. Marius appeals to the Thénardier's daughter, Eponine, to help him find Cosette. Eponine, who is herself secretly in love with Marius, reluctantly agrees.

At a political meeting in a small café, a group of idealistic students prepare for the insurrection. When Gavroche arrives with the news that General Lamarque is dead, the students take to the streets to whip up popular support *("Do You Hear the People Sing?")*. Marius cannot keep his mind off the mysterious Cosette.

Summary of Songs

Look Down

Young Gavroche introduces himself to the audience, and points out his neighborhood in the slums of Saint Michel, in Paris. He shows us two prostitutes who are engaging in a territorial quarrel. A pimp comes along and settles it, and the loiterers in the crowd confer with one another, wondering when the poverty and misery are going to end. They agree that something has to happen soon. Only General Lamarque can speak for the poor. One of the beggars mentions that the general is ill and fading fast. His friend wonders how long it will be till judgment day, before they cut the fat ones down to size, and the barricades arise.

Stars

Javert arrives and sings a monologue in which he talks about his favorite topic: Jean Valjean. He knows he's somewhere out in the darkness, a fugitive running, fallen from grace. He calls God to be his witness when he states that he'll never yield till he and Valjean come face to face. He says Valjean knows his way in the dark, but his own way is the path of the righteous, which is the way of the Lord. He looks up at the stars, appreciating the fact that their multitudes fill the sky with order and light. They are the sentinels, silent and sure, keeping watch in the night. They know their place in the sky and they keep on course, always dependable (like himself). But those who deviate from God's law will fall in flames through the night sky, like Lucifer (once the Bearer of Light and God's right-hand angel). Javert is of the belief that it is written on the doorway of Paradise that those who falter and those who fall must pay the price. Javert would like nothing better than to help God make Jean Valjean pay a spectacular penalty for his "crimes." Meanwhile he will never rest till he sees him behind bars.

Red and Black

A student leader named Enjolras tells his fellow students that they will soon be fighting the National Guard, but they must not underestimate the foe. They need a sign to rally the people, to call them to arms, to bring them in line. The time is 1832, forty-three years after the French Revolution, but the situation in Paris is now worse than ever before. A severe economic crisis had been complicated by a deadly epidemic of cholera. Poverty and misery are rampant, and the people are in despair.

In the midst of all this another student, Marius, shows up and announces that he has fallen in love. This angers his friend Enjolras, who tells the other students that it's time to get serious. They must be clear about the price they might have to pay. The coming insurrection is not just a game for rich young boys to play. The color of the world is changing day by day. He talks about red, the blood of angry men; black, the dark of ages past; red, a world about to dawn; black, the night that ends at last. He probably read Stendhal's *Le rouge et le noir,* a novel first published just two years before the insurrection in 1830, depicting the terrible conditions brought about during the Bourbon Restoration.

Marius is oblivious to the seriousness of the situation at hand. He can only think of the young woman he loves, and he yearns to share his feelings with all his friends. The two young men exchange their views about the symbolism of red and black. Enjolras tells the love-sick Marius that he should turn his attention toward a larger goal, for their little lives don't count at all at this crucial moment in history.

Do You Hear the People Sing?

Enjolras asks the students if they can hear the people sing, singing a song of angry men. It is the music of a people who will not be slaves again. The other students join in the rally during which they all promise to fight for the right to be free. They are excited to think there's a life about to start when tomorrow comes. They are all aware that some will fall and some will live, for the blood of the martyrs will water the meadows of France.

Commentary

Where should we look for freedom?

We can all identify with the students who gather under the leadership of the idealistic Enjolras to protest the tyranny of their feckless government leaders. Four decades have passed since their families made great sacrifices so their children could enjoy a brotherhood of freedom and equality for all, but their hopes were not realized. Corruption in high places has led to poverty and misery in the streets of Paris, and the students are desperate to do something about it. They see themselves as freedom fighters, and one has to admire their bravery, their thirst for justice, and their willingness to lay down their lives for a worthy cause, just as their fathers and grandfathers did before them. But is it really freedom they are fighting for? If they do succeed in bringing down the government, will French citizens really enjoy freedom and justice for all? Unfortunately history has shown that revolutions are often followed either by periods of chaos and confusion or else by even worse tyranny than before, as the new leaders struggle to keep the economy stable. They must fight to maintain order at a time when the vanquished are already plotting to regain power, and hand-rubbing, unscrupulous opportunists like the Thénardiers sprout up from the gutters. Power changes hands, anarchy or tyranny reigns, corruption sets in once again, and freedom takes a holiday.

Yet we know there is something good and right about yearning for freedom and protesting injustices which lead to misery, poverty, and degradation. In Jesus' time the Israelites burned to rid themselves of the Roman conquerers who had taken over their land. The natives were restless, although by and large the Romans were doing a fairly good job of administering this little desert outpost on the far border of their empire. Even so, no country is ever content to be occupied by another, so a political group known as the Zealots began carrying out skirmishes against the hated rulers, but they got themselves crucified for their trouble. They yearned for a strong leader to organize their efforts and show them the way to freedom and glory.

Then along came Jesus, promising living bread and water to anyone hungering or thirsting for righteousness. He offered eternal life to his followers, and as for freedom, he promised this much-coveted and long-sought blessing to all those willing to believe his words, for in this way they would come to know the truth, and the truth would set them free.

The Zealots murmured among themselves. "The *truth* will set us free? Not likely. Ideas like that are for poets— such ideas don't cut the mustard with *us*. We're doers, not dreamers. We'd rather buy our freedom the hard way, the heroic way. The blood of our martyrs will water the sands of Judea!"

Judas Iscariot was a Zealot. Although we know that his betrayal of Jesus was part of God's plan, Judas himself was motivated not so much by the thirty pieces of silver (which he later tossed away) as he was by the desire to overthrow the government by force. Jesus, who advised his followers to be obedient and peaceful and to render unto Caesar what was Caesar's, was a bit of a thorn in his side. How could he rouse his people to sing the song of angry men with this peacenik going around telling them about the kingdom of heaven and other such pie-in-the-sky nonsense? Certainly the hoped-for insurrection would be made a lot easier if this Jesus were put out of the way.

Yet long after Judas's voice was stilled and the Zealots went the way of all flesh, Jesus still lives among us, inspiring us to seek the truth that will ultimately set us free from the cares of everyday life so that we may focus our eyes on our future home. To some this home may sound like a make-believe castle perched somewhere on a distant cloud, but to all those who believe God's promises, that castle is laid on a firm foundation.

Questions

1 *"Look Down":* Some of the angry comments voiced by Beggar 2 bring to mind the words of the thundering God of the Old Testament. Sometimes we learn to understand God better when we personally experience the situations that wound him and grieve him. Compare Hosea 1 (see Bible quote), where God feels hurt by the unfaithfulness he has experienced at the hands of the Israelite nation. He asks Hosea, therefore, to experience how it feels to have an unfaithful wife, so he can then preach to the Israelites with greater passion and conviction.

2   *"Stars":* Javert claims that it is written on the doorway to Paradise that those who falter and those who fall must pay the price. Does this sound scriptural to you?

3   *"Red and Black":* Now that Marius is in love, he believes the world has changed in a burst of light. What do you think he means when he says that what was right seems wrong, and what was wrong seems right? How does his attitude differ now from that of his companions?

4   Enjolras claims that our "little lives" and Marius's "lonely soul" don't count at all compared to the "larger goal" of the popular insurrection. Which do you think is more important? How do circumstances affect us?

5   *"Do You Hear the People Sing?"* How would you feel if your son were describing how the blood of the martyrs would water the meadows of your homeland? What cause is worth dying for?

6   Compare the epiphanies of the Phantom, Aldonza, and Valjean to the Christian experience of being born again.

Bible Quotes

Hosea takes Gomer for a wife

When the Lord began to speak through Hosea, the Lord said to him, "Go, take to yourself an adulterous wife and children of unfaithfulness, because the land is guilty of the vilest adultery in departing from the Lord."

—Hosea 1:2

The Lord said to me, "Go, show your love to your wife again, though she is loved by another man and is an adulteress. Love her as the Lord loves the Israelites, though they turn to other gods…"

—Hosea 3:1

Angels alone that soar above… (see quote below)

Notable Quotes

On freedom:

Stone walls do not a prison make,
Nor iron bars a cage;
Minds innocent and quiet take
That for an hermitage.
If I have freedom in my love,
And in my soul am free,
Angels alone that soar above
Enjoy such liberty.

—Richard Lovelace
To Althea: From Prison
Stanza 4

Chapter Twenty

Young Lovers in Paris

Plot Summary: *Les Misérables* (5)

Now that love has made Cosette more introspective, she asks Valjean to tell her who she is and what happened in her childhood *("In My Life")*. But her adoptive father prefers not to speak about the past, saying that God will reveal the truth to her all in good time.

As Cosette and Marius become better acquainted, we learn that Eponine, the Thénardier's daughter, has been secretly in love with Marius for a long time. When she overhears them expressing their love for each other, she realizes there is no hope for her *("A Heart Full of Love")*.

Out of love for Marius, however, Eponine prevents an attempt by her father's gang to rob Valjean's house. Valjean believes that the men outside in the dark were Javert and his henchmen, so he instructs Cosette to pack her things so they can leave the country right away.

Marius and Cosette are devastated to think they will be separated. In despair, Marius joins his brothers at the barricade. Javert makes his appearance in the middle of all this. He is determined to spy on the students to find out their plans so that he and the other policemen can make the schoolboys "wet themselves in blood." Thénardier and his gang of thieves also show up, hoping to rob the students of their valuables as they fall dead in the streets *("One Day More")*.

Summary of Songs

In My Life

Cosette is amazed that she fell in love with Marius so fast. She wonders if she's been on her own too long. In her life there are times when she catches the sigh of a faraway song that sings of another world just a whisper away. She wonders if Marius feels what she feels, and hopes that he will find her now. Valjean notices her pensive mood, and is sorry that she is feeling lonely with only him for company.

Meanwhile, Marius is at the barricade, where he talks to Eponine about Cosette, who has burst into his life like the music of angels, the light of the sun. His life seems to have stopped as if something is over and something has scarcely begun. He thanks Eponine for bringing them together, for now he is one with the gods and heaven is near. But Eponine loves Marius herself, so every word he says about Cosette is like a dagger in her heart.

A Heart Full of Love

Marius eventually musters the courage to declare his love to Cosette. He doesn't know what to say to her other than to tell her that he is lost, and she replies that she is found.

Eponine overhears them speaking of the brightness of their lives now that they have found each other, and her heart breaks. She chides herself, however, for regretting what was never hers to lose. Marius tells Cosette that with a single look he knew, and she replies that she knew it too. Eponine realizes he will never feel that way about her.

One Day More

Valjean decides he must leave the country with Cosette to keep her safe, for he worries about what will become of her if Javert should manage to find him and put him back in jail. Marius and Cosette are devastated to learn that they must be separated so soon after finding each other. Eponine is in the background, doing what she can to help them, but feeling sad to think about the life that she might have known if he had returned her love. Marius is torn between his desire to leave with Cosette and his duty to fight at the barricade with his friends. He decides he must stay and fight, but the two lovers swear to be true to each other.

Suddenly Javert and the other policemen appear near the barricade, prepared to oppose the "schoolboys" and discover their "little secrets." Thénardier and his gang of thieves also arrive on the scene, ready to steal whatever valuables might come their way. The students sing a naïve, overly-confident song about a new beginning when every man will be a king.

Commentary

What is Love?

This is a question posed by many people down through the ages, and there will probably never be a definitive answer to such a broad topic. Much of it depends on the kind of material we are working with in specific cases, and certainly there are as many different situations as there are people on the earth. We know, however, that love flourishes in ground that is fertile with unselfishness, good character, charity, honor, and self-sacrifice. Jesus said that the greatest love is expressed in the willingness to lay down one's life for the sake of a friend. This does not always or necessarily mean literally dying. It means putting the interest of the loved-one ahead of one's own desires and needs. It means thinking of the other as greater than ourselves. It means filling our hearts with God's spirit and giving it expression.

What, then, can be said of the mysterious emotion two people can suddenly feel when they meet for the first time? Is it love? Yes and no. It has the appearance of love in its powerful feeling and soaring joy. It seems like love in that it fills the heart with noble sentiments and even with a sort of spiritual yearning. But "love at first sight" is a misnomer. Attraction at first sight, yes. It can be an irresistible magnet that pulls two people together, but what are they really to make of each other? What do they know about each other? Why this particular person and not somebody else?

The initial attraction probably has a lot to do with the life experience, emotional needs, and the subconscious yearnings of the two people involved. There's no question that this powerful feeling might eventually lead to love, but in the beginning it acts as the glue that keeps two people together long enough for real love to throw down its roots. If the lovers have the character and the desire to nourish the plant through good times and bad, in sickness and in health, then they will eventually enjoy what Robert Browning so aptly called "the last of life for which the first was made."

The golden years, filled with a life-time of commitment and shared experiences, can indeed be the deepest and most peaceful season in the time allotted to us on the planet Earth. When we speak of a love that has matured like this we often think of an elderly couple as the prototypical example, but Jean Valjean has also dedicated his life to loving and caring for the young orphan, Cosette. He once promised her dying mother that he would "raise her in the light," and he was as good as his word. He had the character and the faith to honor his promise of long ago.

Cosette grew up in miserable circumstances, however, long before Jean Valjean came into her life. The despicable Thénardiers used her as a servant and treated her like scum, while at the same time they fawned over their own daughter, Eponine. But once Valjean and Cosette were together, God continued to bless them and fill their lives with his spirt. The little girl matured into a beautiful young woman who loved and appreciated her adoptive father, but she was also pensive and lonely, with a heart yearning for a love of her own.

Marius filled the bill. We know nothing about his background, but he was just as smitten with Cosette as she was with him. It seemed to them both that theirs was the perfect match, a union made in heaven, and their love radically changed their perspective. Marius lost interest in risking his life for the student insurrection, and Cosette, for her part, was convinced that her life was just beginning. Such is the magic of love in its infancy. Everything is fresh, wondrous, and new. But only God can fully appreciate how tender and vulnerable this precious new life really is, and that is why, perhaps, he often sends his guardian angels to protect young lovers and guide them through the night.

Questions

1 *"In My Life"*: In this song Cosette wonders if people can really fall in love as quickly as she did. What is your opinion? What kind of love is "love at first sight"?

2 *"A Heart Full of Love"*: Eponine is heartbroken when she realizes that Marius is in love with Cosette. How does she deal with her sorrow? How would you expect her to react, given the fact that she has spent her childhood with the Thénardiers?

3 Here Cosette describes the love that she shares with Marius as "a chain they'll never break." This is the third time a chain has been mentioned in *"Les Misérables."* Can you remember the other two?

4 *"One Day More"*: When Marius learns that Valjean and Cosette are going to flee the country, he is torn between following her and staying to fight. What do you think colored his decision to stay (see Lovelace quote →)?

5   What does Thénardier mean when he says, "Watch 'em
    run amok, catch'em if they fall, never know your luck
    when there's a free-for-all"?
6   Javert and Thénardier both, in their own ways, contribute
    to the dreadful conditions in Paris in 1832. Is the student
    insurrection the solution? What would you propose?

Notable Quotes

On honor:
Tell me not, sweet, I am unkind,
That from the nunnery
Of thy chaste breast and quiet mind,
To war and arms I fly.

I could not love thee, dear, so much,
Loved I not honor more.

—Richard Lovelace
To Lucasta: Going to the Wars
Stanzas 1 and 3

On true love:
True love's the gift that God has given
To man alone beneath the heaven:
It is not fantasy's hot fire,
Whose wishes, soon as granted, fly;
It liveth not in fierce desire,
With dead desire it doth not die;
It is the secret sympathy,
The silver link, the silken tie,
Which heart to heart and mind to mind
In body and in soul can bind.

—Sir Walter Scott
The Lay of the Last Minstrel
Stanza 13

Chapter Twenty-One

Unrequited Love

Plot Summary: *Les Misérables* (6)

The students prepare for battle. Marius, noticing that Eponine has joined the insurgents at the barricade, sends her to deliver a love-letter to Cosette. Valjean intercepts the letter outside his house and promises to give it to Cosette. He tries to persuade Eponine not to return to the barricade, but she refuses to listen to his warning. She realizes now that her love for Marius is purely one-sided, and her heart is broken *("On My Own")*.

The students at the barricade are warned by the army that they must give up or die (*"Javert at the Barricade"*). Young Gavroche exposes Javert as a police spy *("Little People")*. The students tie up Javert and leave him sitting on a chair until they have time to decide what to do with him. While approaching the barricade, Eponine is killed *("A Little Fall of Rain")*. She dies in Marius's arms.

The students at the barricade sing a song to days gone by *("Drink With Me")* to lift their spirits. Valjean arrives in search of Marius. Enjolras asks him to guard Javert while he looks for the young man. Valjean is thus given the opportunity to kill Javert, but he shows mercy to his persecutor and allows him to escape. Far from being moved by this act of mercy, Javert hates losing face and becomes more determined than ever to put Valjean in jail.

Meanwhile Valjean prays to God to save Marius from the onslaught that is to come *("Bring Him Home")*.

Summary of Songs

On My Own

Eponine now sings one of the most beautiful, poignant songs in the entire musical score. She is alone again, without a hope, without a friend, and with nowhere else to turn. But the night is near, and she can make believe Marius is with her. When she is on her own she pretends that he's beside her. Without him, she feels his arms around her, and when she loses her way she closes her eyes... and he has found her. Although she knows he can't belong to her, still she says there's a way for them. She loves him, but he is gone again when the night is over. Without him the world around her changes—the trees are bare and everywhere the streets are full of strangers. She loves him, but only on her own.

Javert at the Barricade

The army captain warns the students at the barricade that they're on their own, and nobody will come and help them to fight. He advises them to give up their guns or die. Enjolras angrily accuses him of lying, assuring him that he will see the people rise. Javert, who is pretending to be their scout, arrives with the news that the king has a strong army, so they will need all their cunning to bring them to heel. Enjolras tells him to have faith, for now that they know the army's movements, they'll overcome its power. Javert claims to have overheard their plan, so of course he gives the students false information about the enemy's intentions.

Little People

Young Gavroche suddenly shouts "Liar!" and reveals to the startled students that this so-called scout is really Inspector Javert. He tells Javert that little people aren't easily fooled.

A Little Fall of Rain

The army marches up to the barricade and fires shots. Many students and other young people fall, including Eponine. As she dies in the arms of Marius, she tells him not to fret, for she doesn't feel any pain. He tries to find her some shelter from the rain, but she tells him that a little fall of rain can hardly hurt her now. She's glad to be safe in his arms at last. Marius yearns to close her wounds with words of love, and he assures her that he won't desert her. She's comforted to know that she'll sleep in his embrace, and the rain will make the flowers... Marius finishes her sentence, saying "grow," thus alerting the audience to the fact that Eponine has just passed away.

Drink With Me

In this heart-wrenching song the students gather in the tavern to discuss the purpose of the insurrection and the meaning of their lives. They drink to the days gone by, and wonder if the world will remember them if they fall. They fear that their deaths might mean nothing at all, and that their lives might, in fact, just be one more lie. In a sorrowful aside, Marius says that he doesn't care if he dies now that Cosette will be going overseas. Life without her means nothing to him, and he wonders if she will weep for him if he falls.

Bring Him Home

As the students rest at the barricade on the night before the battle, Valjean watches Marius as he sleeps. He prays to God to spare his life and bring him home safely. He goes on to say that he's like the son he might have known, adding that he would be glad to die in his place, reiterating his plea to let Marius live and to bring him home. Jean Valjean's love for Marius shines through in this song as never before.

Commentary

When love is not reciprocated

No matter how pure and deep one's love may be, there is, of course, no guarantee that it will be returned in kind. There is perhaps nothing so heart-wrenching for a person in love than to discover that the loved-one is interested only in friendship, or is merely toying with the lover.

One of the best examples of the heartbreak caused by an unscrupulous woman who encourages her lover merely for the purpose of satisfying her own vanity can be found in the opera *Carmen* by Bizet, based on a short story by Prosper Merimée. Carmen is a beautiful Spanish *femme fatale* who works in a tobacco factory in Seville (the birthplace of her male counterpart, Don Juan). She leaves a trail of broken-hearted men in her wake as she gleefully prances from one lover to the next in an endless game of conquest. These words from the musical, *Carmen Jones,* describe her *modus operandi* in her own words:

> *You go for me, and I'm taboo,*
> *but if you're hard to get I go for you.*
> *And if I do then you are through, boy,*
> *my baby that's the end of you.*
> *So take your cue, boy,*
> *don't say I didn't tell you true.*
> *I tell you truly, if you love me*
> *that's the end of you.*

In literature as well as in life, this kind of disappointment often leads to despair (as in the case of the young military officer who found himself ensnared in Carmen's trap) or it can inspire the lover to try harder to win the object of his affection. In *The Phantom of the Opera* we noticed how the Phantom used every trick in the book to seduce Christine into succumbing to him, but in the end it was all to no avail. Christine eventually saw through him and chose instead to spend the rest of her life with Raoul, the man who had loved her since her youth and who was willing to lay down his life for her sake.

Does this mean, then, that love's victory is always won by the noble-hearted? Not necessarily. Anybody can lose on the treacherous battlefield of love. In the novel *Don Quixote de la Mancha,* the well-meaning knight-errant threw himself body and soul into a series of adventures in order to become worthy of his lady's love. But it was all in vain—the lady was more interested in the welfare of her pigs than in the plight of the knight who so desperately loved and wooed her. The hapless knight made a rather poor choice. His love had blinded him to the emotional and spiritual limitations of his lady, so in the end, his spirit crushed, he went home to die.

In the musical version, however, Wasserman decided to make the prostitute Aldonza capable of being profoundly changed by Don Quixote's love. Even though the knight still expired in the end, as all of us must, we nevertheless had the satisfaction of witnessing how Aldonza was made into a new creation by her knight's unswerving and unconditional love. We were also able to rejoice as she and Sancho Panza sallied forth to continue their master's quest after he died.

And what about Eponine? How does she fit the picture? In spite of having the worst possible role-models as parents (the comically off-putting Thénardiers), Eponine's love for Marius is strong and unselfish (an excellent case against genetic predisposition and in favor of free will). She sacrifices her own yearning for happiness in order to bring him together with Cosette, the woman he loves, and in so doing she lays down her life for him, both figuratively and literally. We mourn the death of a young person who could yet find happiness (in spite of what she believes at the time), but unfortunately in literature it is almost a plot requirement that the arrows of *eros* lead either to soaring heights of joy or to the black pit of despair. In real life, however, *eros* keeps lovers together while *agape* slowly grows in their hearts.

Questions

1 *On My Own:* Eponine spends a lot of time on her own, living in her head and imagining that she and Marius are together. Do you think these habits of mind and heart are likely to prepare her well for everyday life and for the hum-drum (and sometimes harsh) realities of marriage?

2 *Javert at the Barricade:* Not only does Javert relish the idea of seeing the students "wet themselves in blood," but he tries to lull them into a false sense of security by telling them there will be no attack that night. There is an old saying that states that all is fair in love and war. Do you think this is true?

3 *Little People:* Because of their inexperience, young folks are often the most enthusiastic about war ("we'll fight like twenty armies and we won't give up"). Compare Gavroche's bravado with Valjean's prayer *(Bring Him Home).* Who has more courage, the person who charges ahead with no knowledge of the likely consequences, or the one who is frightened to death but fights anyway?

4 *A Little Fall of Rain:* It has long been a romantic idea that the only solution to passionate love is either separation or death. After all, a nine-to-five job and three screaming children hardly seem a fitting end for a passionate love involving two noble, poetic souls. Do you think that we should help our young people learn to distinguish a little better between passionate, romantic love and the kind of love that has greater staying-power? Or should we just relax in the knowledge that *eros* will lead to *agape* if the lovers have what it takes?

Chapter Twenty-Two

Overweening Pride

Plot Summary: *Les Misérables* (7)

The next day the students send little Gavroche to get some more ammunition, and he is shot. By the end of the day almost all the rebels are killed, including Enjolras. Jean Valjean escapes into the sewers, carrying the wounded, unconscious Marius. After running into Thénadier, who is robbing the corpses of the rebels, he emerges into the light only to come face-to-face with Javert. He pleads for time to deliver the young man to a hospital. Javert reluctantly allows him to go. His pride and his sense of righteous superiority were shattered when he was exposed to the mercy of this lowly "criminal." He feels there is no place for him in the light-filled world of Jean Valjean, so he throws himself into the River Seine *("Javert's Suicide")*.

The women of Paris mourn the gratuitous death of the young rebels, remembering how they all had mothers who once cradled them tenderly in their arms. Their grief fills them with cynicism and bitterness against God ("what's the use of praying if there's nobody who hears?").

Marius feels guilty that he is the only one left living, and he sings a lyrical song filled with passionate sorrow as he ponders the death of his friends *("Empty Chairs")*. They fought for a better tomorrow, but Marius believes now that their sacrifice was in vain, for they never saw the dawn of the new day they fought so valiantly to achieve.

Dog Eats Dog

The Thénardiers are roaming around down in the sewers, stealing all the valuables from the corpses. They tell the audience that someone's got to collect their odds and ends as a service to the crown. They steal a ring from Marius who is lying there unconscious, but they don't recognize him. As far as the Thénardiers are concerned it's a dog-eat-dog world, where God is in his heaven calmly ignoring the tragic action unfolding in the world below. They claim that "he [God] don't interfere 'cause he's as dead as the stiffs" at their feet. They raise their eyes to see the heavens, and only the moon looks down.

Javert's Suicide

When Javert witnesses Valjean's concern for the wounded Marius, he reflects on the mercy that the ex-convict also showed to him (Javert) at the barricade when he let him go free instead of killing him as he had been instructed to do by the students. Valjean had his chance to wreak vengeance on him, but instead he showed him pity and charity. Could it be that his legalistic, rule-driven attitude toward wrongdoers might be a great deal less pleasing to God than the unselfish, compassionate actions of that scum of the earth, Valjean? He fights the thought that he might be morally inferior to his nemesis, reminding himself that he is the law, and the law is not mocked. He is determined to spit his pity right back into his face, for he can't bear the thought that this desperate man whom he has hunted for so many years should now hold dominion over him. It particularly galls him to think that after all this effort on his part, Jean Valjean's sins should be forgiven and his crimes go unpunished.

"Must I now begin to doubt?" he asks himself. Doubt is always a very threatening and fearsome condition, and Javert knows this better than anyone. He knows his heart is stone, but yet it trembles. "Is he from heaven or from hell?" he asks himself regarding Valjean. "Does he know that granting me my life today, this man has killed me even so?"

Javert, who demanded so much strength and perfection from others, crumbles under the load of his doubt and shame. The stars look black and cold as he stares into the void of a world that cannot hold—the world of Jean Valjean.

He looks down into the blackness of the waters of the Seine, and realizes there is nowhere he can turn and no way to go on, so he lets himself be swallowed up and consumed by the cold void reflected in the unfeeling river.

Turning

The women of Paris speak of the pointlessness of the young men's fight for justice, for now they are lying lined up side by side in the street. Someone used to cradle them and kiss them when they cried, they say, but who will awaken them now? They were schoolboys fighting for a new world that would rise up like the sun, but where's that new world now, they ask, now the fighting's done? It's the same old story, they say, and they believe that there is no use praying, for there's nobody who hears.

Empty Chairs

After the failed insurrection, Marius returns to the old café where he used to meet with all his friends in days gone by. "There's a grief that can't be spoken," he declares, his heart filled with sorrow. "There's a pain goes on and on... Empty chairs at empty tables, now my friends are dead and gone." He can hear them now, talking about revolution and singing about tomorrow, but tomorrow never came. He asks his friends to forgive him for still being alive when they are all dead and gone. He doesn't know what their sacrifice was for... all they have left are empty chairs and empty tables where his friends will sing no more.

Commentary

A glimpse of heaven and hell

God gave us the freedom to make our choices, for better or for worse. It would appear, however, that we are too limited to understand the enormous importance of the here and now and the tremendous implications of the decisions we make in our short life-spans here on earth. It could be said that both heaven and hell begin here in our own lives and then slowly intensify as they stretch into eternity. What starts out as an unselfish life dedicated to the worship of God and to the welfare of others eventually becomes a life of utter bliss and a joy so profound it defies description.

On the other hand an individual who, for any number of reasons, refuses to accept God's saving grace is likely to discover that he is his own worst enemy. At first he is merely the person he has always been when he reaches the doorstep of eternity, but then he creates his own hell as he grows more and more isolated and lonely, lost in a spiritual void with no light at the end of the tunnel.

Jesus wanted to save us from this kind of fate. His most impassioned exhortations were warnings to us not to choose the road leading to death and destruction. His disciples may have been slow sometimes to understand what he was telling them, but one thing was perfectly clear to all of them: hell was definitely not where they wanted to go. It is a place of utter darkness, devoid of the loving presence of God, a black hole in the fabric of time where there is no hope of finding a wormhole to another existence.

Some people ask what it is they need to be saved *from.* It would appear that hell might be something to consider. To be lost in space, alive and conscious of the alternatives that were so lightly and proudly rejected (and with what self-confidence!), is not a destiny that would appeal to very many of us.

Questions

1 In *"Dog Eats Dog,"* Thénardier states that life in the sewer is a breath away from hell. Elaborate.

2 In the same song Thénardier states that God is dead. Where is such thinking likely to lead?

3 *"Javert's Suicide":* Why do you think Javert takes his own life? What is his destiny likely to be? What caused him to make this choice? How might his ideas have been altered?

4 *"Empty Chairs":* In this song we're told that the students' self-sacrifice was for naught. Marius, the sole survivor, feels an indescribable grief when he contemplates the situation. How do our words or actions sometimes put in question Christ's sacrifice for us? Do you think that this causes God a grief so profound that "it can't be spoken?"

5 Keeping in mind the observations that were made in the Commentary, why do you think our lives here on earth are so precious and so important? Would it be fair to say that we (and others) are living at the crossroads of our destinies?

6 What names do the Greeks give to the two faces of love as described in the first Notable Quote on the next page?

7 Which characters in Les Misérables fit the description of the two faces of love?

8 Comment on the second Notable Quote.

Notable Quote

Two Faces of Love

Love seeketh not itself to please,
Nor for itself hath any care,
But for another gives its ease,
And builds a Heaven in Hell's despair.

Love seeketh only self to please,
To bind another to its delight,
Joys in another's loss of ease,
And builds a Hell in Heaven's despite.

William Blake
The Clod and the Pebble
Stanzas 1, 3

Notable Quote

Words on a T-shirt worn by a customer at the Brewery Market, Halifax, Nova Scotia:

Front:
   "God is dead."
             — Nietsche

Back:
   "Nietsche is dead."
             — God

Chapter Twenty-Three

Mr. and Mrs. Marius Pontmercy

Plot Summary: *Les Misérables* (8)

When Marius recovers from his injuries, he asks Valjean for Cosette's hand in marriage. Valjean decides it is time to confess everything about his past to his future son-in-law, who up to this point does not realize that it was he, Jean Valjean, who saved his life down in the sewers. He humbly tells Marius that because he is a convict on the run, he must go away after their wedding rather than taint the sanctity and safety of their union.

At the wedding festivities *("Beggars at the Feast")* Thénardier attempts to blackmail Marius, claiming that Cosette's future father-in-law is a murderer. As proof he produces a ring that he stole from a "corpse" in the sewers on the night the barricades fell. It turns out to be Marius's own ring, so the young man realizes it was Valjean who saved his life that night (Valjean had already recounted how he had found a wounded man in the sewer and carried him to safety).

He and Cosette go to visit Valjean, and she learns for the first time of her own history as Valjean dies, joining the spirits of Fantine, Eponine, and those who died on the barricades. *("Valjean's Death")*

Summary of Songs

Beggars at the Feast

The "Baron and Baroness de Thénard" arrive at the wedding feast to pay their respects to the bride and groom, and to have some fun hobnobbing with the upper crust. They gleefully boast about how easy it is to cheat and steal from these decent, law-abiding folks who are too trusting to hang onto what they've been given in life.

Valjean's Death

In contrast to the raucous, triumphant song that is belted out by the humorous yet despicable Thénardiers, Jean Valjean's final song is a touching and heartfelt goodbye to the people he has loved the most. He is on his deathbed, and Cosette is by his side. He tells her he can die in peace now, knowing that she's safe in the arms of Marius.

Cosette assures her father that he's going to live, for it's too soon to say goodbye. Valjean promises to try to live for her sake, but he goes on to say that he has written down his last confession for her to read while he is "sleeping." It's the story of those who always loved her, and how her mother gave her life for her and entrusted her to his care.

At this point Fantine appears to Valjean. She will guide him to heaven where chains will never bind him, and where all his grief will be behind him. She asks God to look down on him in mercy. Valjean, in turn, asks God to forgive him all his trespasses and take him to his glory.

Eponine joins Fantine in this vision, and Jean Valjean asks them to take his hand and lead him to salvation. He bids them take his love as well, for love is everlasting. In his last words he asks them to remember the truth that once was spoken, that to love another person is to see the face of God.

Finale

The students who died at the barricade gather around and sing about the people who are climbing to the light: "For the wretched of the earth there is a flame that never dies." Even the darkest night will end and the sun will also rise. They will live again in freedom in the garden of the Lord... the chain will then be broken and they will all have their reward. The students tell the others that somewhere beyond the barricade there is another world that beckons with distant drums, heralding a better world that awaits them when tomorrow comes.

Commentary

Heaven and hell revisited

C.S. Lewis (1898-1963) was a gifted writer on the subject of Christianity. He was an inspired novelist, poet, academic, literary critic, essayist, and Christian apologist who taught at both Oxford and Cambridge. He is perhaps best known for his fictional works such as *The Screwtape Letters* and *The Chronicles of Narnia,* and for his many books on Christian apologetics—especially *Mere Christianity.*

One of his most intriguing books is *The Great Divorce,* which describes an ordinary man who dies one night and wakes up in a tavern surrounded by his drinking buddies. Everyone is having a jolly time, and the man assumes he has gone to heaven. But as time goes by he has some unpleasant altercations with his acquaintances and he feels very ill done by, believing that he deserves to be in a better place than this tavern, wherever it is.

God has mercy on him and allows him to go to heaven, but the man feels even more at odds with the people there, who strike him as being too willing to please and perhaps a little too cloyingly joyful for his taste—the sort of people who like to sing and dance and scatter flowers. He never takes the time to get to know them on a deeper level, nor does he feel moved by their general kindness, their desire to be of service, and their understanding of some of the more important concepts in the universe. As far as he is concerned they are not "interesting" people, and he believes he has little in common with them.

He begins to feel bored and a bit lonely. God allows him to go back to hell where he prefers to be, and the fighting continues until he can't stand the sight of his buddies any longer. He ends up living in eternal isolation, gnashing his teeth over the many slights and insults and bad treatment he has endured, and blaming God for messing up. He complains about how unfortunate he is not to have encountered anyone, either above or below, who is worthy of his attention.

"Hell," as Jean Paul Sartre once put it, "is other people."

Questions

1   Do you think we choose our own destinies? Compare the different views of Christianity embraced by Javert and Valjean.

2   Comment on the following statement from *The Great Divorce*: "Those that hate goodness are sometimes nearer than those that know nothing at all about it and think they have it."

3   To whom might this quote from *The Great Divorce* apply in *Les Misérables?* "Good beats upon the damned as incessantly as sound waves beat on the ears of the deaf, but they cannot receive it. Their fists are clenched, their teeth are clenched, their eyes fast shut. First they will not, in the end they cannot, open their hands for gifts, or their mouth for food, or their eyes to see."

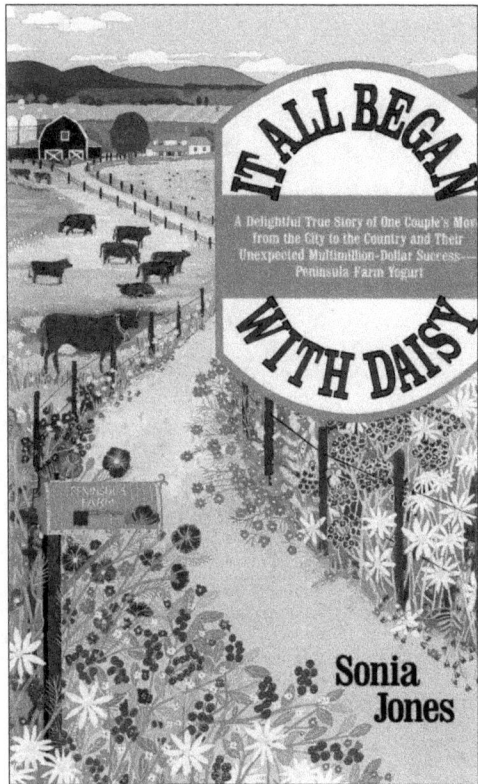

If you enjoyed reading *What is Love?,* you will also like *It All Began with Daisy* (Dutton/Penguin, New York, 1987). When Sonia Jones moved with her husband to Nova Scotia to teach at Dalhousie University, they bought an oceanside farm and settled down to enjoy a life of quiet contemplation. But they bought a cow in an unguarded moment, and their tranquility evaporated overnight. Daisy quickly became the head of the household, providing them with more milk than they knew what to do with. They started making yogurt for a local health food store, eventually becoming a multi-million dollar corporation.

Featured as an alternate selection by the *Literary Guild of America,* condensed by *The Reader's Digest,* translated into 15 languages, and circulated worldwide to 28,000,000 readers.

Available on Amazon or at www.erserandpond.com

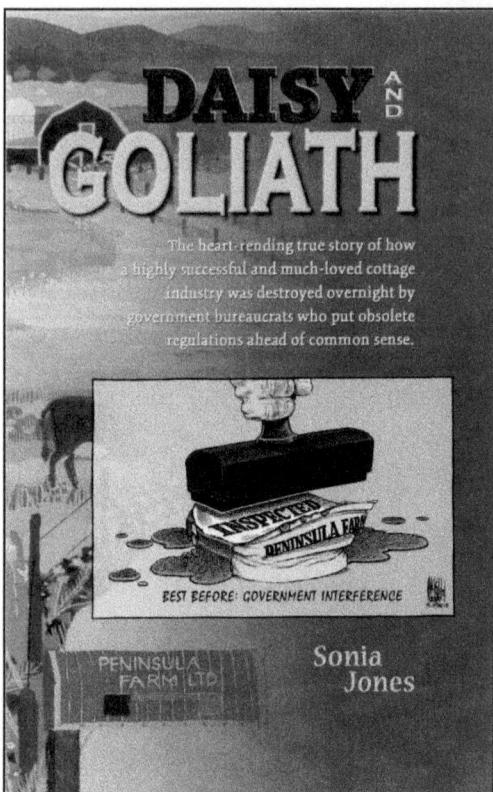

If you enjoyed reading *It All Began with Daisy,* you will also like *Daisy and Goliath* (Erser and Pond, 2007), the sequel to *It All Began with Daisy,* which describes the vandalism of Peninsula Farm by agents of the federal government. It is an informative, intelligent, and sometimes painfully humorous inside look at the struggles of one family to run a highly successful small business in spite of the current trend toward the industrialization and the corporatization of farming.

Available on Amazon or at www.erserandpond.com

The

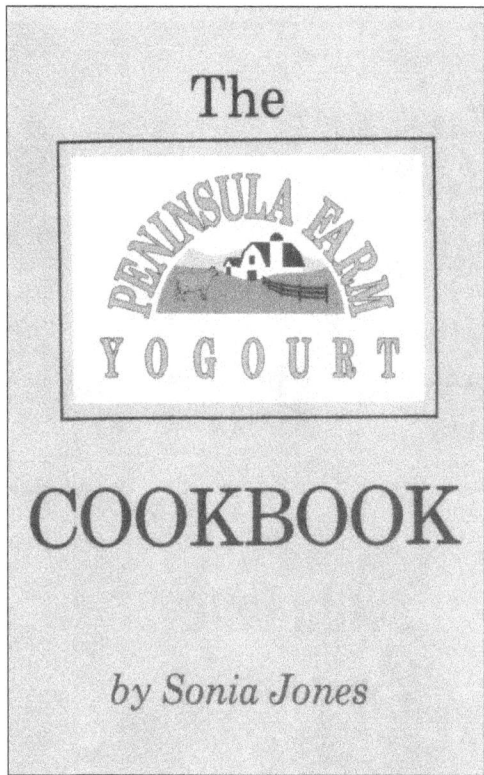

PENINSULA FARM

YOGOURT

COOKBOOK

by Sonia Jones

If you have ever wanted to make your own yogurt at home, this is the book for you. Sonia Jones, a highly successful yogurt-maker for twenty-five years, reveals her tried-and-true recipes along with instructions on how to make delicious yogurt (and what to do when you fail). This well-loved book is a compendium of yogurt fact, yogurt lore, yogurt recipes and all you need know to become part of the yogurt revolution. Published by Pottersfield Press, Nova Scotia

Available on Amazon or at www.erserandpond.com

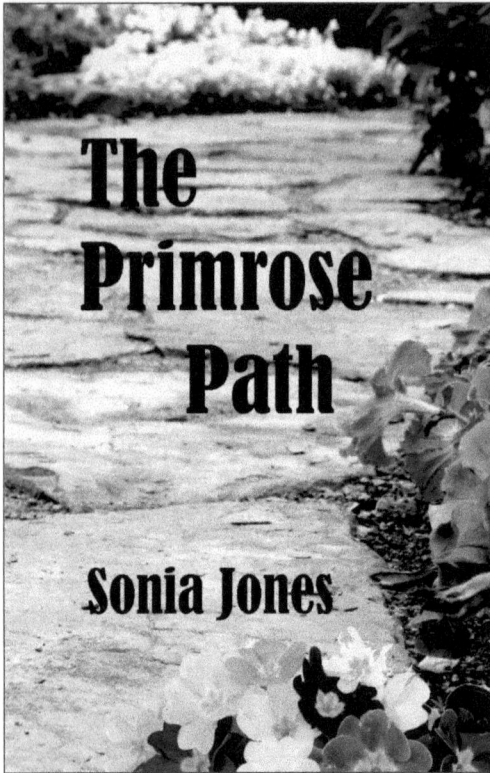

The Primrose Path

Sonia Jones

The Primrose Path (Erser and Pond, 2008) is the true story of Percy Pond, the author's grandfather and celebrated photographer who documented the Klondike Gold Rush, the founding of Juneau, and the culture of the native tribes in Alaska. It also introduces the author's father, Kay Harrison, who was the Managing Director of Hollywood's Technicolor Films in Paris, London, and Rome. He often traveled to Spain as well, where he conferred with producers such as Sam Bronston, who made *John Paul Jones* in Technicolor, and Mike Todd who, before his death in 1958, was planning to produce a Technicolor   film about Don Quixote.

Available on Amazon or at www.erserandpond.com

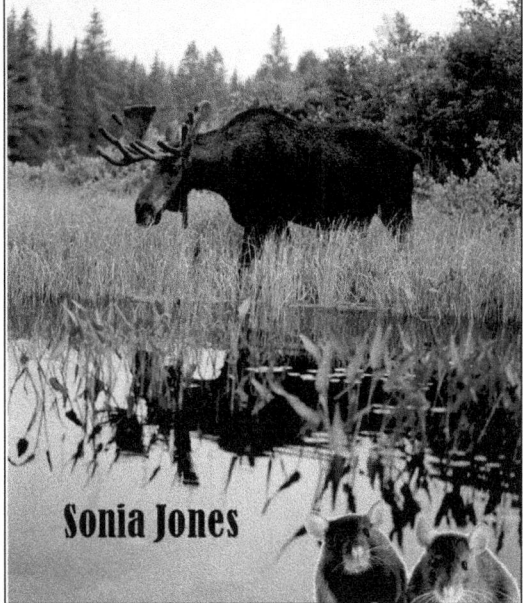

Of Mice and Moosecalls

Reflections on life ever laughing

Sonia Jones

AVAILABLE IN COLOR OR BLACK AND WHITE

If you enjoyed reading *The Primrose Path,* you will like *Of Mice and Moose Calls* (Erser and Pond, 2008), a beguiling collection of Sonia Jones's humor columns published in *The Banner.* The topics range from warbling church mice to operatic moose calls, and from chaos on the farm to wild roosters running amok in the Dutch countryside. Described by New York Times critic Robert Coleman as having "a born teacher's eye for the well-chosen example," Sonia Jones' humorous and poignant stories are sure to move you.

Available on Amazon or at www.erserandpond.com

CLONING JESUS

COLOR EDITION

Sonia Harrison Jones

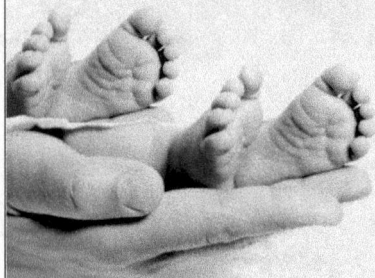

AVAILABLE IN COLOR OR BLACK AND WHITE—IN
ENGLISH AND IN SPANISH OR FRENCH TRANSLATIONS

If you enjoyed reading *Of Mice and Moose Calls,* you will also
like *Cloning Jesus* (Erser and Pond, 2009), available at Erser or
Amazon in the color edition (with over 100 color images), or save
$8.00 when you buy the black-and-white edition without photos.

WHAT READERS ARE SAYING: I LOVED it! For me the test
of a good book is that when I'm not reading it I'm thinking about it
and trying to figure out when I will be able to get back to it, and
that definitely happened with this book. – Julie Graveline, retired
Canadian Naval officer

This is a masterpiece! It was a real gripper. My wife and I almost
fought for the computer. There is much in this book about
"intellect apologetics" —the tragedy of using Christianity to gain
power. The last chapter of Cloning Jesus highlights "living
apologetics." Great!
—Rev. Clarence Vos, pastor and retired professor, Calvin College

Available on Amazon or at www.erserandpond.com

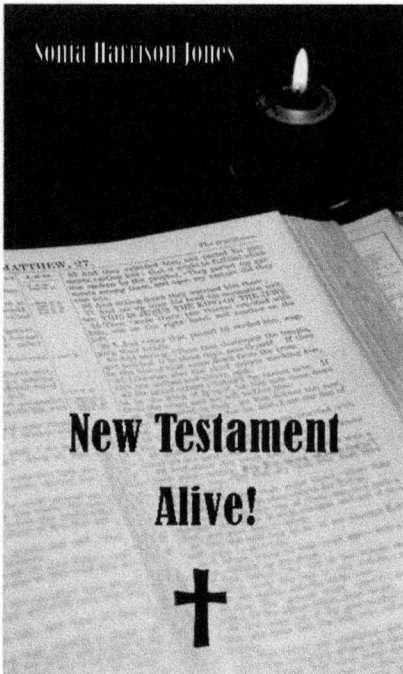

The Choir

Sonia Harrison Jones

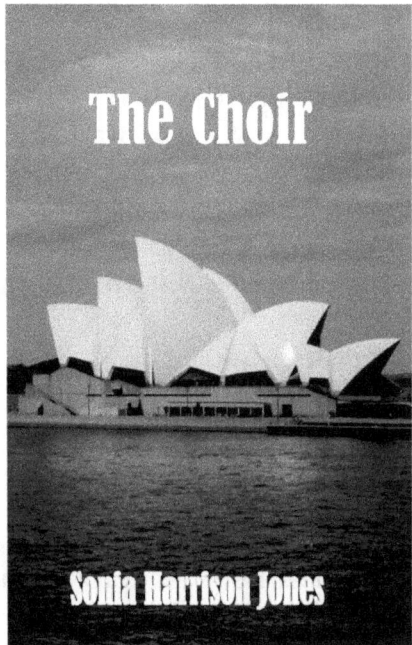

This is an unusual mystery novel where lurking danger combines with inspiring Broadway songs, providing sensitive insights into the human condition. The plot includes two love stories and the choir's once-in-a-lifetime performance at the Sydney Opera, leading to a poignant and uplifting finale.

What readers are saying

This is a must read. Dr Jones displays great storytelling ability and crafts a tale of suspense, intrigue and humor bundled with romance and existential issues related to self-worth and purpose. —Dr Michael R Lawrence, neuropsychologist, MI

I was intrigued by this novel right from the opening chapter. I was led through a gripping story, beginning with unintentional identity theft and then on to the high seas, with rich characters forging deep connections through serendipity and chemistry. I didn't put the book down until I had savoured the epilogue's satisfying revelations. A terrific read! —Janet Manuel, poet and choral singer, Nova Scotia

Available: Amazon, Kindle, or at www.erserand pond.com

BOOKS BY SONIA HARRISON JONES
PUBLISHED DURING HER TENURE
AT DALHOUSIE UNIVERSITY

SPANISH ONE, VAN NOSTRAND, NEW YORK, NY, 1974
SPANISH ONE, 2ND EDITION, 1979
(adopted by over 100 universities in the US and Canada)

ALFONSINA STORNI, GK HALL, BOSTON (TWAYNE WORLD AUTHORS), 1979. Biography of Argentine poet, playwright, and short story writer (author won Canada Council grant to research the project in Buenos Aires) Second printing will be published in 2013.

Sonia (Harrison) Jones has been listed in *Who's Who in the East, International Authors and Writers Who's Who, The World Who's Who of Women, and Who's Who in Canada*

ABOUT THE AUTHOR

Sonia Harrison Jones was born in England and educated in the U.S. After receiving her PhD from Harvard University in Romance Languages and Literatures, she chaired the Spanish Department at Dalhousie University in Halifax, Nova Scotia, Canada for many years.

She and her husband bought a cow in an unguarded moment, but Daisy's bountiful milk production was too much for their little family to handle. So they began a small yogurt business which eventually became a multi-million dollar enterprise. The corporation was so successful that the feds found a way to regulate it right out of existence.

Now Dr Jones is well into her third career, writing books a mile a minute. She has published a dozen books in various genres, and is looking forward to writing many more. For further information please go to www.erserandpond.com.

www.ingramcontent.com/pod-product-compliance
Lightning Source LLC
Chambersburg PA
CBHW061726020426
42331CB00006B/1118